THIRD EDITION

COUNSELING STRATEGIES AND INTERVENTIONS

Harold Hackney, *Fairfield University*

L. Sherilyn Cormier, *West Virginia University*

PRENTICE HALL, ENGLEWOOD CLIFFS, NEW JERSEY 07632

Library of Congress Cataloging-in-Publication Data

Hackney, Harold, [date]
   Counseling strategies and interventions.

   Rev. ed. of: Counseling strategies and objectives. 2nd
ed. c1979.
   Includes bibliographies and index.
   1. Counseling.   I. Cormier, L. Sherilyn (Louise
Sherilyn)   II. Hackney, Harold.
Counseling strategies and objectives.   III. Title.
BF637.C6.H25 1988   158'.3   87-13699
ISBN 0-13-183328-6

Editorial/production supervision and
   interior design: Serena Hoffman
Cover design: Diane Saxe
Manufacturing buyer: Carol Bystrom

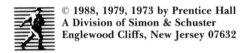

© 1988, 1979, 1973 by Prentice Hall
A Division of Simon & Schuster
Englewood Cliffs, New Jersey 07632

Printed in the United States of America

10   9   8   7   6   5   4   3   2   1

ISBN 0-13-183328-6   01

PRENTICE-HALL INTERNATIONAL (UK) LIMITED, *London*
PRENTICE-HALL OF AUSTRALIA PTY. LIMITED, *Sydney*
PRENTICE-HALL CANADA INC., *Toronto*
PRENTICE-HALL HISPANOAMERICANA, S.A., *Mexico*
PRENTICE-HALL OF INDIA PRIVATE LIMITED, *New Delhi*
PRENTICE-HALL OF JAPAN, INC., *Tokyo*
SIMON & SCHUSTER ASIA PTE. LTD., *Singapore*
EDITORA PRENTICE-HALL DO BRASIL, LTDA., *Rio de Janeiro*

Contents

Exercises

Preface

In the hiatus since the second edition of this book, the counseling profession has shown remarkable signs of life, strength, and growth. Emergence of the "professional counselor" identity is particularly apparent, both in the literature and in professional organizations. This identity has undoubtably been accelerated by the establishment of training standards that have come from the Council for Accreditation of Counseling and Related Educational Programs (CACREP) and by the increased number of training programs accredited by the American Psychological Association. These standards have identified the complex array of skills that are expected of a professional counselor, and they call for the inclusion of a supervised training experience in the form of an on-site counseling internship, in addition to the more traditional practicum experience. This emphasis on direct experience draws attention to yet another dimension of professional training, that of clinical supervision. The Association for Counselor Education and Supervision has focused upon this activity, with the result that increasing numbers of training institutions are incorporating supervisor training in their programs.

Despite all these changes, we also acknowledge that there is much that has not changed during the past few years. The relationship between counselor and client, the communication process, the cognitive, affective, and behavioral nature of client problems, the counselor's influence in the helping process, the client's influence, and the palette of counseling interventions from which the counselor selects—all of these remain as enduring aspects of the counseling process.

An adequate textbook must attempt to blend the old with the new, to illustrate how counseling has evolved while maintaining its essential character. We have set this blending as our goal in this edition. The reader will note a number of additions and changes that reflect the evolving complexity of the counseling profession. Chapter One identifies the context of professional counseling: who the professional counselor is and what kinds of activities the professional counselor enters. This context includes a wide variety of roles and functions. It might even seem to the untrained eye that the differences among helpers are greater than the similarities. We attempt to dispell that impression in Chapter Two, where we discuss the helping relationship. It is this helping relationship that proves to be the unifying force for disparate roles and functions.

Although the helping relationship connotes a sense of shared purpose, there is an added expectation for the counselor, the expectation that the counselor be both responsible and responsive in exploring the client's needs and concerns. In Chapters Three through Eleven we identify the skills and interventions expected of a beginning professional counselor. Some of these skills are rudimentary; others are more advanced and require coaching and practice. Chapters Three and Four define the counselor's responsibility to be aware of and responsive to the client's communication patterns. Effective attending skills place the counselor in a responsible role in the counseling relationship. This responsibility is examined in Chapter Five, dealing with session management.

Chapters Six through Eight delineate the basic counseling strategies designed to elicit, support, or direct client change. Whether the focus be the client's thoughts, attitudes, or feelings, or more likely, a combination of all three, the counselor has certain tools or skills that facilitate the client's growth. Often these skills enable the counselor to understand the client's problem or the client's world.

Chapter Nine is a pivotal point in the book. Titled Conceptualizing Problems and Setting Goals, it builds upon the fundamentals of the early chapters and is the foundation for the remaining chapters of the book. Although the counselor is instrumental in conceptualizing problems (usually with the assistance of a particular theoretical orientation), the goal-setting process is inherently dependent upon *mutual* discussion and agreement between counselor and client. Drawing upon mutually accepted counseling goals, the counselor begins the most crucial portion of the relationship, the focus upon overt change. This calls for more than relationship skills, more than active listening. There are many counseling interventions—derived both from theory and practice and supported by research—that are synonymous with effective counseling. In Chapters Nine through Eleven, we explain and suggest classroom activities that will help the reader to understand and begin practicing these interventions.

Finally, we have included a chapter on the process of clinical supervision and how beginning counselors may use it to advance their skills. The content of this chapter is entirely new. Counselor educators have long used clinical supervision skills in the training of counselors, but the specificity of those skills and the inclusion of the trainee as a participant in successful clinical supervision has not been dealt with in most professional texts.

As you begin the process of understanding the role of helper, and as you acquire the necessary skills required for effective helping, you will come to realize that the ultimate goal is to develop your abilities to the point that they are a natural extension of your existing interpersonal skills. But this will not be the case in the beginning. The interventions and even the conceptualizations may seem unnatural, inconsistent with your existing behaviors, or inappropriate. As you become more accomplished in the craft of counseling, these counseling skills will begin to feel more comfortable, appropriate, and effective. Ultimately, they will become a natural part of your professional practice.

Harold Hackney
L. Sherilyn Cormier

CHAPTER ONE

The Helping Profession

The helping profession includes a broadly knit collection of professionals and paraprofessionals, each fitting a particular need or segment of society. Some are directly identified as helping professionals, such as psychiatrists, psychologists, professional counselors, marriage and family therapists, and social workers. Others are professionals from other disciplines who enter the helping network for temporary periods of time. Most notable among these are ministers, physicians, nurses, and teachers. When we talk about the helping profession, we must keep this fluid interplay between career helpers and peripheral helpers in mind. The bond they share in common is a desire, a need, or even a mission to be of help. This helping activity has both a subjective and an objective quality and can be studied from both perspectives.

Most counseling textbooks devote at least a portion of one chapter to the subject of helping. You might think that a process so inherent to human nature as this act of extending oneself to another person should be self-evident. And yet we continue to belabor the subject in ways not unlike the poet who talks about love. In a psychotherapeutic context, the process has carried many labels, among which are *treatment, analysis, facilitation*, and *modification*. In the company of such terms, the label *helping* seems innocently harmless, if not simplistic. In fact, the act of helping proves not to be so simple or clear to the participant or observer.

WHAT IS HELPING?

The process of helping has several dimensions, each of which contributes to the definition of *helping*. One dimension specifies the conditions under which helping occurs. Another dimension specifies the preconditions that lead one person to seek help and another to provide help. Yet a third dimension relates to the results of the interaction between these two persons.

Helping Conditions

The conditions under which helping occurs are quite complex, but in their simplest terms may be described as involving "(a) someone seeking help, (b) someone willing to give help who is (c) capable of, or trained to help (d) in a setting that permits help to be given and received."[1]

The first of these conditions is obvious; one cannot help without the presence of someone seeking help. If I don't want to be helped, nothing you can do will be helpful. If I'm not sure I want to be helped, then perhaps you will be helpful, provided you can enjoin me to make a commitment to accept help.

The second condition requires the willingness or intention to be helpful. Here it would be good to differentiate between the *intention* to be helpful and the *need* to be helpful. Many would-be helpers are driven by the need to be helpful and use the helping relationship for their own ends. This is rarely a conscious act. Neediness has a way of camouflaging itself in more respectable attire. But when the relationship is dictated by the helper's needs, the possibilities for helping are minimal.

The third condition reflects the counselor's skills, either learned or natural. It is not enough to be well intentioned if my awareness and my behaviors drive people away. The fourth condition, a setting in which help may occur, refers to the physical surroundings in which the helper and help seeker meet. Conditions such as privacy, comfort, aesthetic character of the room, and timing of the encounter all contribute to the setting in which helping transpires.

Carl Rogers has discussed the "necessary and sufficient conditions" for helping to occur.[2] His description includes conditions similar to those listed above. But he also adds some personal qualities of the counselor (accurate empathy, unconditional positive regard) and a communication issue: that the client be able to perceive the counselor's understanding and respect for the client.

Preconditions to Helping

Of course, the helping process doesn't occur in a vacuum. Both the helper and the person seeking help bring a history to the relationship. For the client, that history includes coping skills, problem-solving abilities,

---

[1] L. Sherilyn Cormier, and Harold L. Hackney, *The Professional Counselor: A Process Guide to Helping* (Englewood Cliffs, N.J.: Prentice-Hall, 1987), p. 1.
[2] Carl Rogers, "The Necessary and Sufficient Conditions of Therapeutic Personality Change," *Journal of Counseling Psychology* 21 (1957): 95–103.

self-concept issues, temperament, and interpersonal experiences. A deficiency in any one of these areas can produce obstacles to the helping process. Similarly, the helper's experience in the helping role, and his or her personal self-concept, professional demeanor, interpersonal experiences, and self-awareness affect the development of the relationship. A deficiency in any of these helper areas can also produce obstacles to the helping process.

There is more to the issue of preconditions than just the characteristics of the helper and client. The client's intentions in seeking help, the types of change the client wishes to accomplish, the level of commitment to working and change are preconditions as well. Some clients come to counseling with the expectation that others must change. For other clients, change is a means to an end, and the end may conflict with the helper's values. In other words, the type of change sought by the client is one that the helper cannot endorse. There are also clients who view the helping relationship as an alternative to change. For them, the relationship may extend over months or even years with very little movement from the original complaints. Yet the periodic contact with a helper provides a sense of dealing with their problems, while at the same time ensuring minimal commitment to growth.

When we take both the conditions and the preconditions of helping into account, we can begin to construct a definition of what the helping process is. Clearly it must include personal qualities of both the helper and the client, relationship qualities that influence the interaction between the two, professional qualities that relate to the competencies of the helper, situational qualities that affect the progress of the relationship, and client objectives. Each of these qualities will be examined in greater detail in future chapters.

Results or Outcomes

It seems almost pointless to say that helping has not transpired if neither the helper nor the client see the experience as helpful. It is true that the two may have differing views of the outcome. If the helper views the experience as helpful but the client does not, then one has to raise serious questions about the efficacy of the event. On the other hand, if the client views the experience as helpful but the helper does not, then the experience may be termed helpful. It is at this point that we must acknowledge the relativity of the helping relationship. Some relationships are extraordinarily helpful, while others are almost totally unhelpful. Most helping relationships fall somewhere between these two extremes. A specific helper may have a variety of helping experiences with different clients that range from minimally to significantly helpful. This variation is explained by all of the factors we have discussed thus far. Certain combinations of factors produce minimal outcomes even for the best of helpers. Because of this, it becomes apparent that the more a helper knows about past successes with certain client patterns and problems, the better that helper may serve a particular client.

WHO ARE HELPERS?

To this point, we have not used the label *counselor*. That is because not all helpers are counselors, and not all counselors are helpers. But, for the remainder of this book, we shall refer to the helper as a counselor, having qualified the term, and with the acknowledgement that there are many other job labels that also identify the helper, such as *psychiatrist, psychologist, social worker, priest, minister, rabbi.*

There are also different strata of counselors. These strata might be labeled the *nonprofessional*, the *paraprofessional*, and the *professional*. Nonprofessional helpers are all around us. They are acquaintances who come to wakes, neighbors who show up to help when conditions become overwhelming, friends who call to see why we haven't been seen lately, and even strangers who listen and give a moment of understanding when problems become oppressive. Nonprofessional counselors are also members of the local Weight Watchers Club, Alcoholics Anonymous, and other self-help groups. The common ingredients among nonprofessional helpers are compassion, an ability to extend themselves beyond their own needs, and communication/listening skills.

Paraprofessional counselors possess these same qualities of the nonprofessional counselor. But in addition, they have received formal training, usually directed toward a specific type of problem or specific type of setting in which clients may be seen. While they do not possess certificates or licenses, they are recognized in the helping professions and perform valuable services. Examples of paraprofessional counselors include psychiatric aides, mental health technicians, crisis center hotline volunteers, and church youth workers.

Professionals include the psychiatrist, who has combined a medical school background with a residency in psychiatry; the psychologist, who has combined doctoral-level training in psychotherapy with an internship in psychotherapy; the professional counselor, who has combined a master's or doctoral degree with practicum/internship experiences in a counseling setting; and the social worker, who has combined a Master of Social Work (M.S.W.) degree with internship training. We also include the school guidance counselor, the family therapist, the mental health counselor, the agency counselor, the rehabilitation counselor, the substance abuse counselor, the career counselor, and the corrections counselor, all of whom have received postgraduate training and have met certain certification standards.

Yet another way professional counselors may be distinguished from paraprofessionals is by their affiliation with certification boards or commissions. Some are licensed or certified by state boards of health service providers, state psychology boards, or state counselor boards. Some are certified by national commissions such as the Academy of Certified Social Workers, the National Board of Certified Counselors, the American Association for Marriage and Family Therapy, or the American Association of Pastoral Counseling. In each of these examples, certain criteria have been met, examinations passed, interviews held, and credentials scrutinized before the person is admitted to membership.

WHERE DOES HELPING OCCUR?

If we take into account the nonprofessional helper, then helping can occur wherever two or more people might meet. But for our purposes, with focus on the paraprofessional and professional helper, the locations tend to be institutionalized; that is, they tend to be in settings that reflect continuing and ongoing service delivery. Furthermore, they tend to be located close to specific target populations for which they are intended. The following discussion of representative settings and the services they perform will provide some sense of the helping spectrum.

School Counselors

School counselors are found in elementary, middle or junior high schools, and high schools. Elementary school counselors do provide some individual counseling with children, but they are more likely to work with the total school environment. Much of the elementary school counselor's focus is on working with the teaching staff to construct a healthy psychological environment in the school for young children. This is accomplished through teacher conferences, classroom presentations, parent conferences, and talking to the children.[3]

Middle school and junior high school counselors share this total school perspective but tend to spend more time with students, individually and in groups, and somewhat less time with teachers and parents. This slight shift in focus reflects the developmental changes that are occurring with preteens, who find themselves involved in self-exploration and identity crises.

Counseling in the high school reflects a noticeable shift to the student as individual. Career and college planning, interpersonal concerns, family concerns, and personal identity issues tend to dominate the student's awareness, and the counseling process attempts to provide an environment in which these issues may be addressed. The counselor's day is therefore much more task oriented. Some students are referred by teachers, but many students are self-referrals. The high school counselor often works with student groups on career and college issues, but individual contact is the main medium for other concerns. Counseling sessions often are no more than thirty minutes long, and the typical relationship is intermittent rather than continuous.

College Counselors

Most college counseling occurs in counseling centers or psychological services centers. A wide variety of problems are addressed, including career counseling, personal adjustment counseling, crisis counseling, and substance abuse counseling. College counselors also see students with mild to severe pathological problems ranging from depression to suicide gestures

---

[3] Merle M. Ohlson, ed., *Introduction to Counseling* (Itasca, Ill.: F. E. Peacock, 1983), pp. 133–44.

to eating disorders. In addition to individual counseling, much reliance is placed on group counseling and on training paraprofessionals to run crisis telephone services and peer counseling programs. In writing about this population, Utz has noted that many of the problems of adult life have their beginnings at the college age. As a result, "the college counselor has an opportunity to help students when problems would seem more manageable and subject to change."[4]

College counselors require considerably more training in individual and group therapy than do high school counselors. Many college counselors have a doctorate in psychology. Those who do not are likely to be skilled in specific areas of psychotherapy.

Counseling in Community Settings

Counselors working in community settings usually are master's degree–level social workers (M.S.W.) or mental health counselors (M.A.). Their places of employment are the most diverse of all counseling settings. They "may be in private practice or they may be employed in one of a variety of community agencies, ranging from the large community mental health center with a staff of specialists trained to deal with many types of situations, to the small one- or two-person office which has limitations to the types of clients it serves."[5]

Family service agencies, youth service bureaus, satellite mental health centers, YWCA counseling services, substance abuse centers, and a variety of religious counseling centers are examples of what one finds in community settings. Much of what is done is psychotherapy, whether with individuals, families, or groups. In addition, the community counselor may become involved in community advocacy efforts and direct community intervention. The types of problems seen by community counselors encompass the spectrum of mental health issues. The clients include children, adolescents, adults, couples, families, and the elderly. In other words, community counselors see an enormous variety of clients and problems in a typical month. The work demands are often heavy, with case loads ranging from twenty to forty clients per week.

Counseling in Religious Settings

Counseling in religious settings is in many ways similar and in some ways different from that in other counseling settings. The religious counseling center often is associated with a particular denomination (for example, Catholic Family Services, Methodist Family Counseling Center, Jewish Family Services). The similarities include the range of individual and family problems seen, the types and quality of therapy provided, and the counse-

[4] Patrick W. Utz, "Counseling College Students," in *Introduction to Counseling*, ed. Merle M. Ohlsen (Itasca, Ill.: F. E. Peacock, 1983), p. 169.
[5] Ohlsen, *Introduction to Counseling*, p. 297.

lors' professional qualifications. The differences reflect the reasons why some religious groups establish their own counseling services. There is at least some acknowledgement of the role of religion or God in the individual's life problems. Many religious counselors believe that human problems must be examined and changes introduced within a context of religious beliefs and values. The religious counseling center is undeniably attractive for many clients who, because of their backgrounds, place greater trust in the counselor who works within a religious affiliation.

Counselors in religious settings often are ordained ministers who have obtained postgraduate training in counseling. But increasing numbers of the laity are also entering religious counseling settings. Their training may be similar to that of the community mental health counselor or the marriage and family therapist.

Counseling in Industrial Settings

Many professionals consider the private sector to be the new frontier for counseling services. Forrest describes this movement as a response to industry's need to deal with employee personal problems that negatively affect job performance.[6] Counseling services occur primarily in the form of Employee Assistance Programs (EAPs) that are administered either within the plant or through a private contract with a counseling agency. EAPs are occurring with increasing frequency in businesses, industries, governmental units, hospitals, and schools.[7] While the primary focus of most EAPs is the treatment of substance abuse problems, some have expanded into other types of personal and family problems.

In addition to employee assistance programs, a new type of counseling service has appeared in industry settings: the outplacement counseling service. *Outplacement* refers to the process of facilitating the transition from employment to unemployment or from employment in one corporation to employment in another. The need for outplacement counseling is increasing as corporations streamline their operations to cut costs or to address new goals and objectives. The client may be a top executive, middle manager, line foreman, or laborer. Counseling takes the form of career counseling and includes the administration of career and personality inventories. The objective for management clients is to provide data and counseling that will help executives assess their career options and develop plans for obtaining new positions, and to support clients through that transition period. The objective for plant employees who may be affected by plant closings is to identify career alternatives for the employee and to assist the company in designing retraining programs that will help the unemployed worker to obtain a new job. Much that is done in outplacement counseling is similar to what the career counselor would do. But the outplacement counselor is usually a person who has worked in an industry

---

[6] Donald V. Forrest, "Employee Assistance Programs in the 1980s: Expanding Career Options for Counselors," *Personnel and Guidance Journal*, 62, no. 2 (1983): 105.

[7] Ibid.

setting and understands the characteristics of this clientele from firsthand experience.

WHAT ARE THE INGREDIENTS OF PROFESSIONAL COUNSELING?

We have described four settings in which professional counseling occurs. There are many others, of course, including marriage and family therapy, rehabilitation counseling, correctional institution counseling, employment counseling, and geriatric counseling. In all of these settings, and with the variety of presenting problems that are seen, there is a common core of counselor characteristics, skills, and abilities. These common ingredients may be categorized as the personal qualities of the counselor, the counselor's interpersonal skills, the counselor's discrimination or conceptual skills, and the counselor's intervention skills.

The Counselor's Personal Qualities

What are the raw materials, the predisposing conditions that contribute to development of a highly skilled counselor? Do all counselor trainees possess these raw materials? Corey, Corey, and Callanan have observed that "a counselor's values, beliefs, personal attributes, life experiences, and way of living are intrinsically related to the way he or she functions as a professional."[8] They identify nine personal qualities that are found in effective counselors:[9]

1. Good will . . . sincere interest in the welfare of others
2. The ability to be present for others; the ability and willingness to be with them in their experiences of joy and pain
3. A recognition and acceptance of one's personal power; being in contact with one's own strength and vitality; without need to diminish others or feel superior to them
4. The knowledge that one has found his or her own counseling style, that style being an expression of one's own personality
5. A willingness to be vulnerable and to take risks
6. Self-respect and self-appreciation; a strong sense of self-worth
7. A willingness to serve as models for their clients
8. A willingness to risk making mistakes and to admit having made them
9. A growth orientation

The Counselor's Interpersonal Skills

Although the personal qualities listed above are basic ingredients for good counseling, possession of these qualities alone does not ensure that one will be a successful counselor. There is a second level of characteristics

[8] Gerald Corey, Marianne Schneider Corey, and Patrick Callanan, *Issues and Ethics in the Helping Professions*, 2nd ed. (Monterey, Calif.: Brooks/Cole, 1984), p. 24.
[9] Ibid., pp. 24–27.

that determine how the counselor is able to relate to others. Egan describes some of these qualities as the ability to "translate" what one reads into something that would work; possession of good common sense and good social intelligence; willingness to work hard with clients; skill at helping clients explore the world of experience, feeling, and behavior; action orientation; and being "at home" with people, both one-to-one and with groups.[10] Other interpersonal skills include the ability to listen and to communicate accurately what one has heard without becoming dominant in the interaction, and being able to communicate one's competence, trustworthiness, and sensitivity to the other person's situation. This array of characteristics must contribute to a general ability to put clients at ease, to elicit client trust, and to work through difficult moments, difficult tasks, and difficult problems.

The Counselor's Discrimination/Conceptualization Skills

As the counseling relationship evolves, the counselor becomes increasingly involved in the client's personal world. From the client's perspective, the counselor *becomes* part of his or her world. This involvement challenges the counselor to be in the relationship and yet to remain objective. Such a challenge is very difficult because it requires the counselor to exhibit congruence, honesty, and professional responsibility, all at the same time.

The counselor must be able to listen, to comprehend, to relate, to think through, to recognize connections and contradictions, to conceptualize what these might mean within some theoretical framework, to react, to instigate, to support, to challenge, and to empathize—all within the span of a counseling session. And this must all be done as believably as it is felt. Otherwise, the counselor will take on a phony or incongruent persona.

The Counselor's Intervention Skills

Finally, counselors must be able to implement their conceptualization of what would facilitate the client's growth and success with presenting problems. It is our belief that "all counselors, regardless of theoretical orientation, have a therapeutic plan that they follow, a plan that is related to the assessment of the presenting problem, to their view of human nature and change processes, and to the resulting goals that have been agreed upon."[11] These interventions may address the client's feelings and attitudes, the client's thought processes and assessments of life situations, the client's behaviors or efforts to change, or the client's interpersonal relationships and the effect those relationships have.

Some intervention skills are nothing more than good common sense

[10] Gerard Egan, *The Skilled Helper: A Systematic Approach to Effective Helping* (Monterey, Calif.: Brooks/Cole, (1986), pp. 28–29.

[11] Cormier and Hackney, *The Professional Counselor*, p. 25.

and are as common among friends as they are in counseling. Other interventions are unique to the therapeutic relationship and are formed out of the theoretical conceptualizations of human relationships. As counselors grow in experience and training, their repertoire of intervention skills grows, and their ability to recognize when and how to introduce interventions increases.

HOW ARE PROFESSIONAL COUNSELORS TRAINED?

We have already indicated that professional counselors are trained in graduate programs, usually affiliated with higher education institutions, that lead to a master's degree. Traditionally these programs required thirty-three semester credits, but recently many of them have been upgraded to require forty-eight to sixty semester credits. These latter programs may be designed to meet professional criteria established by the Council for Accreditation of Counseling and Related Educational Programs (CACREP).

Most training programs begin with a series of courses that introduce the helping professions, settings, client populations, and professional ethics. Early in most programs a counseling techniques laboratory or prepracticum introduces students to communication skills and entry-level counseling interventions, and provides opportunities to try out these skills in an observable setting (either through two-way mirror or closed-circuit video). Such a course includes content that is presented in this text. Typically, this course is followed by a counseling practicum in which students work with real clients under the supervision of a skilled counselor or therapist. That supervision may include live observation, videotaped review, or audiotaped review. Whatever the medium, sessions are reviewed by the supervisor, and feedback is provided to the trainee to permit assessment and professional growth.

Concurrent with these courses, most students take courses in group counseling (sometimes including a group practicum), psychology, educational and psychological testing, and career counseling and development. Toward the end of the program, many trainees are required to complete a one-year internship in a counseling setting related to their program. This may be in school counseling, agency counseling, college counseling, or another related setting. Programs in social work and marriage and family therapy differ in some of the didactic content, but the experiential portions are similar.

SUMMARY

We have attempted to examine the meaning of helping in the context of human problems and who the helpers are. Professional helpers are found in many settings and encounter a wide variety of human problems. The effective helper brings to the setting certain personal qualities, without which the client would not likely enter into the alliance in which help occurs. But more than personal qualities are necessary for one to be a professional helper. One must possess certain interpersonal skills, conceptual skills, and intervention skills to be an effective counselor. While the exact parameters of these skills may be defined by the counselor's theoretical orientation, there is no denying that the effective counselor has them and the ineffective counselor does not.

In the chapters that follow, we shall examine these skills and provide you with exercises and discussion questions to help in your integration of the material. Chapter 2 will look at the helping relationship and conditions that enable it to develop in positive directions to facilitate the client's progress. Chapters 3, 4, and 5 address the interpersonal skills of the counselor in regard to attending to clients, recognizing communication patterns, and managing the counseling session. Chapters 6, 7, and 8 focus on the cognitive and affective messages of clients and ways in which counselors can differentiate between and respond to these two types of messages. Chapters 9, 10, and 11 address the counselor's skills in conceptualizing problems and selecting and implementing strategies and interventions. Finally, Chapter 12 looks at the special issues involved in supervisor-trainee sessions, with the aim of helping the beginning counselor to make full use of the benefits of supervision.

DISCUSSION QUESTIONS

1. In a small group of three to five class members, each member should identify a preferred setting in which he or she would choose to be a professional counselor. Discuss among yourselves why you chose the particular setting. Does it have to do with your personal qualities? Your perception of the demands of the setting? Your perception of the "rewards" of working in that setting?

2. Now choose a second-most-preferred setting (other than your first choice). Continue the discussion as directed in Question 1. How did you find your reactions to be different in this second discussion? What might you learn from these differences? Did you perceive the other group members as having similar or different reactions to the second choice? What did you learn about them as a result? Share your reactions candidly.

3. Identify a person you have known who was, in your opinion, an exceptional helper. What qualities did this person possess that contributed to his or her helping nature? How do you think these qualities were acquired? Do you have any of these qualities?

RECOMMENDED READINGS

FORREST, DONALD V.,   "Employee Assistance Programs in the 1980s: Expanding Career Options for Counselors," *Personnel and Guidance Journal* 62, no. 2 (1983): 105–107.

Forrest provides an in-depth analysis of the Employee Assistance Plan movement in industry, its philosophy and components, and its implications for professional counselors.

NUGENT, FRANK A.,   *Professional Counseling, An Overview*. Monterey, Calif.: Brooks/ Cole, 1981.

Nugent offers a good overview of the field of professional counseling. His discussion of the nature and demands of different counseling settings is well worth reading.

OHLSEN, MERLE M.,   ed., *Introduction to Counseling*. Itasca, Ill.: F. E. Peacock, 1983.

Ohlsen is one of the pioneers of professional counseling. His description of the history and trends, modes of counseling delivery, and target populations is excellent. Chapters written by other authors describe the special demands of counseling women, blacks, and the aged.

CHAPTER TWO

The Helping Relationship

Much of what is accomplished in counseling is dependent upon the quality of the relationship. In all the writing on this subject, none offers more than the person-centered approach does. This approach is described by Boy and Pine (1982):

> A relationship exists when there is a mutual interaction of persons and a reciprocal human exchange. Two subjects, counselor and client, form the essence of a third subject—the relationship—that is, the totality of what goes on concurrently in the counselor and the client and between the counselor and the client. Client behavior has a reciprocal impact on counselor behavior, which in turn has a reciprocal impact on client behavior.[1]

The person-centered approach derives principally from the work of one individual, Carl Rogers. Rogers emerged on the counseling scene at a time when two psychological approaches, psychoanalysis and behaviorism, were dominant. Through his influence, the profession began to focus upon the relationship between therapist and client, as opposed to the existing emphasis upon either the client's intrapsychic experience or patterns of behavior. In one of his early writings, Rogers defined what he believed to be the "necessary and sufficient conditions" for positive personality change to occur.[2] These conditions referred to characteristics inherent in a constructive interpersonal relationship, including accurate empathy, unconditional positive regard, and genuineness. These concepts have evolved over the years, and today they are generally acknowledged by most theoretical approaches as core conditions in the therapeutic process.

---

[1] Angelo V. Boy and Gerald J. Pine, *Client-Centered Counseling: A Renewal* (Boston: Allyn and Bacon, 1982), pp. 130–131.
[2] Carl Rogers, "The Necessary and Sufficient Conditions of Therapeutic Personality Change," *Journal of Counseling Psychology* 21 (1957): 95–103.

In addition to these core conditions, the helping relationship has an intentional dimension. Hansen, Stevic and Warner describe this intentional nature as:

> . . . an alliance formed to help the client move toward a goal: more appropriate behavior. The client is able to try changes through an internalization of this therapeutic alliance. The internalization is made possible by the counselor's acceptance of the client as a person and by the former's help in resolving a problem.[3]

In this chapter we shall examine the helping relationship, taking into account both the core conditions and the notion of intentionality.

ACCURATE EMPATHY

Rogers defined empathy as perceiving "the internal frame of reference of another with accuracy and with the emotional components and meanings which pertain thereto as if one were the other person, but without ever losing the 'as if' condition."[4] In the decade following Rogers's definition, twenty-one additional definitions of empathy could be documented in the counseling literature alone.[5] Even with such variety, there remains a surprising amount of agreement among counseling professionals. Accurate empathy implies just this: that your sense of the client's world fits his or her self-image. This gives clients the feeling that you are "in touch" with them.

Empathic understanding involves two primary steps:

1. Accurately sensing the client's world; being able to see things the way he or she does
2. Verbally sharing your understanding with the client

How do you know when the client feels you have understood? Client responses such as "Yes, that's it" or "That's exactly right" indicate some sort of recognition by the client of the level of your understanding. When your clients say something like that after one of your responses, you are assured that they feel you are following and understanding what is occurring.

Learning to understand is not an easy process. It involves the capacity to switch from your own set of experiences to those of your clients, as seen through their eyes, not yours. It involves sensing the feelings they have, not the feelings you had or might have had in the same or similar

---

[3] James C. Hansen, Richard R. Stevic, and Richard W. Warner, Jr., *Counseling: Theory and Process*, 4th ed. (Boston: Allyn and Bacon, 1986), p. 234.

[4] Carl Rogers, "A Theory of Therapy, Personality, and Interpersonal Relationships as Developed in the Client-centered Framework," in *Psychology: A Study of a Science, Vol. 3: Formulations of the Person and the Social Context*, ed. S. Koch (New York: McGraw Hill, 1959), p. 210.

[5] Harold Hackney, "The Evolution of Empathy," *Personnel and Guidance Journal*, 57, no. 1, (1978): 35.

circumstances. It involves skillful listening, so that you can hear not only the obvious, but also the subtle shadings of which, perhaps, even the client is not yet aware.

The first step in developing the art of accurate empathy is to acknowledge your good intentions, to indicate that you *want to understand* your client. Can you remember your own feelings when someone really seemed to understand what you were saying? Or when someone completely misunderstood an experience you shared? Occasional misunderstanding is, of course, inevitable in any relationship, including the counseling one. Although it is never as helpful as complete understanding, it is still desirable to convey your desire and effort at understanding, as in the following interaction:

Counselor: "If I heard you correctly, you seemed to be really questioning your ability and even your desire to love."
Client: "No, that wasn't quite how I meant it."
Counselor: "I would really like to understand this. Will you share a little more of it with me?"

Can you recall a relationship in which your own strong feelings prevented you from hearing the feelings of the other person? Some counselors' efforts at understanding the client are blocked because their own strong needs to be heard and understood interfere. Developing accurate empathy also means identifying and resolving your own needs so that they do not interfere with your responding to and understanding the feelings and concerns of your client.

Understanding alone is not sufficient. You also must express verbally to clients your sense of understanding about them. This kind of communication is, in effect, a kind of mirror—feeding back clients' feelings to them, without agreeing or disagreeing, reassuring or denying. Accurate empathy involves not only mirroring the client's feelings but also some parts of the immediate process. For example, if clients continually ask many questions, rather than discussing the issues that brought them to counseling, it would be appropriate to reflect on the obvious with statements such as:

"You have a lot of questions to ask right now."
"You seem to be wanting a lot of information about this."
"You are asking a lot of questions. I wonder if you are uncertain about what to expect."

Learning to develop accurate empathy with your client and with other people takes time and practice. You must "experience the [client's] feeling, first, comprehend it as best you can, then react to it."[6]

EXERCISES: ACCURATE EMPATHY

In the following exercises see what you can do to *hear* the client accurately and to communicate your perceptions to the client.

[6] Hackney, "The Evolution of Empathy," p. 37.

A. Hearing and Verbalizing Client Concerns

Using triads with one person as speaker, a second as respondent, and the third as observer, complete the following tasks. Then rotate roles until each person has had an opportunity to react in all three ways.

1. The speaker should begin by sharing a personal concern or issue with the listener.
2. The respondent should
   a. listen to the speaker;
   b. verbalize to the speaker what he or she heard.
3. The observer should note the extent to which the others accomplished their tasks and whether any understanding or misunderstanding occurred.

Following a brief (five-minute) interaction, respond verbally to the following questions:

Speaker: Do you think the respondent heard what you had to say? Did you think he or she understood you? Discuss this with respondent.

Respondent: Did you let the speaker know you understood or attempted to understand? How did you do this? What blocks within yourself interfered with doing so?

Observer: Discuss what you saw taking place between the speaker and respondent.

Now reverse roles and complete the same process.

B. Understanding Client Concerns

This exercise should be completed with a small group of people sitting in a circle (at least three, but no more than ten).

1. Each participant is given a piece of paper and a pencil.
2. Each participant should complete, in writing and anonymously, the following

   sentence: My primary concern about becoming a counselor is _____

   _____

   _____

3. Papers are folded and placed in the center of the circle.
4. Each participant draws a paper. (If one person receives his or her own, all should draw again.)
5. Each participant reads aloud the concern listed, then talks several minutes about what it would be like to have this concern. Other participants can then add to this.

This process continues until each participant has read and discussed a concern. When discussing the concern, attempt to reflect only your *understanding* of the world of the person with this concern. Do *not* attempt to give a solution or advice.

After the exercise, members should give each other feedback about the level of empathic understanding that was displayed during the discussion. Sometimes it is helpful to have all group members rank each other as to who showed the most understanding, who showed the least, etc. Feedback should be specific so participants can use it for behavior change.

POSITIVE REGARD

In his early writings, Carl Rogers described positive regard as unconditional.[7] That quality has been interpreted by Hansen, Stevic and Warner as "respect(ing) the client regardless of differences in values, differences in how one sees the world; in short, no condition is set upon the client's behaviors and experiences."[8] Lietaer observes that this is "probably one of the most questioned concepts in client-centered therapy," noting that "there is a potential conflict between genuineness or congruence on the one hand and unconditionality on the other."[9] Perhaps for this reason, more recent writers have relabeled positive regard as "nonpossessive warmth."

Positive regard, or nonpossessive warmth, is often misconstrued as agreement or lack of disagreement with the client. Instead, it is an attitude of valuing the client. To show positive regard is to express appreciation of the client as a unique and worthwhile person.

Think for a few moments about several of your existing relationships. Choose those that you would describe as good interpersonal relationships. Also think about a few poor ones. Can you determine any missing elements in the latter relationships? Chances are your feelings about the other person in the good relationships are more positive. Liking another person has a circular effect. When you value clients, your sense of liking will be communicated to them; this alone will enhance their feelings for themselves and add to their appreciation of themselves as worthwhile human beings. Counselors typically discover that a better relationship exists with those clients they describe in positive terms. Think now of one of your clients (or a friend) with whom you have some difficulty relating. How do you describe this person? Is it primarily a positive or negative description? If you said "negative," you are focusing on the individual's *limitations*. Sometimes this has to be expressed to the client (or friend) in order to permit feelings of positive regard to develop. Think again of the same person. This time, identify two or three strengths of the person. Sometimes thinking of a client in this way can increase your sense of positive regard.

---

[7] Rogers, "The Necessary and Sufficient Conditions," p. 98.

[8] Hansen, Stevic, and Warner, *Counseling*, p. 112.

[9] Germain Lietaer, "Unconditional Positive Regard: A Controversial Basic Attitude in Client-centered Therapy, in *Client-Centered Therapy and the Person-Centered Approach: New Directions in Theory, Research, and Practice*, eds. Ronald F. Levant and John M. Shlien (New York: Praeger, 1984), p. 41.

EXERCISES: POSITIVE REGARD

A. Overcoming Barriers to Positive Regard

Think of expressing to the client (1) those limitations that may be blocking your sense of liking for the client, and (2) those strengths that increase your appreciation for the client. The following steps may assist you in expressing this:

1. Picture the other person in your mind. Begin a dialogue in which you express what it is that is interfering with your sense of positive regard. Now reverse the roles. Become the other person. What does the person say in response? Then what do you say?
2. Complete the above process again. This time express the strengths you see in the other person, what you appreciate about that person. Again reverse the roles. Become the other person. What does he or she say in response? Then what do you say?

This exercise can be used with any client toward whom you have difficulty experiencing positive regard.

B. Expressing Positive Regard

Take a few minutes to think of a person with whom you are currently in relationship and for whom you experience positive regard. What kinds of things do you do to express your feelings of positive regard for this person? Jot them down.

_____

_____

_____

_____

There is no set answer to the exercise above, because each person has a different style of communicating good feelings for another person. The first step, though, is positive regard—to feel comfortable enough to *express* warm feelings to someone else. Being free enough to spontaneously share feelings of regard for another human being is a process that can be learned.

Think again for a moment about several of your existing relationships with a few people close to you—perhaps your spouse, parent, child, neighbor, or friend. Then respond, in writing, to the following questions:

What is your level of expression of positive regard to these people?

How often do you say things like "I like you"; "It's nice to be with you"; "You're good for me"; "I enjoy you"; and so forth?

What is your feeling when you do?

What is the effect on the other person?

If your expression of these kinds of statements is infrequent, what might be holding you back?

Either now, or later, seek out someone you like and try to express these kinds of feelings to the other person. Then think again about the above questions. Share your reactions with your partner.

In doing this you will probably note that warmth and positive regard are expressed both nonverbally and verbally. Nonverbally, they are shown by facial expression, smiling, and eye contact. In fact, you might think of your entire nonverbal stance as communicating a degree of enthusiasm for the other person.

In counseling, positive regard is sometimes shown when the physical posture of the counselor mirrors that of the client. Verbally, you express your feelings for another person by statements that reflect a sense of caring and affection, best described, perhaps, by the word *nurturance*. Affectional nurturing statements can have a strong effect on the client and on the relationship. They are most effective when used *selectively* and *sincerely*. You know the feeling you have about someone who is always saying nice things—these statements lose their effect when used constantly.

Some examples of affectional nurturing statements are:

Client: "I know I shouldn't do that because at those times I'm selfish, yet it's hard for me to always do everything for her first, but I am selfish and that's an even worse way for me to be.

Counselor: "I like you even when you're selfish."

Client: (Crying) "I'm sorry I'm crying. They (parents) tell me I am a baby for doing it, but I am so worried, but uh, I'll try not to do it."

Counselor: "It's all right for you to cry with me."

Think of some affectional nurturing statements on your own. List them below and discuss them with someone.

_____

_____

_____

_____

_____

GENUINENESS

The notion that the counselor should project genuineness in the interview has also been difficult to define. Rogers tended to connect it with *congruence*, a condition reflecting honesty, transparency, and openness to the client. Rogers and Truax described counselor congruence in the following way:

In relation to therapy, [congruence] means that the therapist is what he *is*, during the encounter with the client. He is without front or facade, openly being the feelings and attitudes which at the moment are flowing in him. It involves the element of self-awareness, meaning that the feelings the therapist is experiencing are available to him, available to his awareness, and also that he is able to live these feelings, to be them in the relationship, and able to communicate them if appropriate. It means that he comes into a direct personal encounter with his client, meeting him on a person-to-person basis. It means that he is *being* himself, not denying himself.[10]

The beginning counselor may find this condition easier to apply in theory than in practice. Questions such as "What if I really don't like my client? Should I let that be known? Wouldn't it destroy the relationship?" rise inevitably when genuineness and congruence are examined. And the appropriate answer to these questions may not be entirely satisfying. Genuineness dictates that the counselor be honest, but in helpful, rather than destructive, ways.

There is much more to genuineness than the occasional encounter with a disagreeable client. Many beginning counselors fall into the trap of "playing the counselor's role" by merely reflecting the client's feelings. Limiting your expression and involvement to this set of responses presents several problems:

1. It creates insecurity; the client is kept in a constantly ambiguous state about how you feel.
2. There is no role-model effect for the client. If you can effectively express *your* immediate feelings, it encourages the client to do likewise.
3. There is no source of feedback other than the client's perceptions. Expression of your feelings gives clients an idea of how they are perceived by others.

Expression of your feelings should not take precedence over understanding the client's feelings. The counseling relationship does not have all the mutuality present in many other relationships, such as friend to friend, husband to wife, and so forth. Sharing your feelings is most beneficial when it serves one of the three purposes mentioned above.

Before you can express your feelings, you must become aware of them. Ask yourself, for example, what it means to be genuine. Can you tell when you are being yourself, or when you are presenting an image that is different from the way you actually feel? In order to communicate genuineness to the client, you must first learn to get in touch with yourself and your feelings—to become aware of who you are as an individual and what kinds of thoughts and feelings you have. This involves learning to discriminate between your various feelings and allowing them to come into your awareness without denial or distortion; it means for example, that when you are happy you can acknowledge that you are happy, or that when you are angry you can be aware of your anger.

To assist you in becoming aware of your own thoughts and feelings, pick a partner and spend a few minutes with each other in the dyadic

---

[10] Carl Rogers and Charles B. Truax, "The Therapeutic Conditions Antecedent to Change: A Theoretical View," in *The Therapeutic Relationship and Its Impact*, ed. Carl R. Rogers (Madison, Wis.: University of Wisconsin Press, 1967), p. 101.

encounter exercise.[11] All you need to do is respond to the open-ended questions as honestly and directly as possible. Both of you should respond to one question at a time.

EXERCISE: DYADIC ENCOUNTER

This dyadic encounter experience is designed to facilitate getting to know another person on a fairly close level. The discussion items are open-ended statements and can be completed at whatever level of self-disclosure one wishes.

> My name is _____
> The reason I'm here is _____

One of the most important skills in getting to know another person is listening. In order to get a check on your ability to understand what your partner is communicating, the two of you should go through the following steps one at a time:

Decide which one of you is to speak first in this unit.

The first speaker is to complete the following item in two or three sentences:

> When I think about the future. I see myself. . .

The second speaker repeats in his or her own words what the first speaker has just said. The first speaker must be satisfied that he or she has been heard accurately.

The second speaker then completes the item in two or three sentences.

The first speaker paraphrases what the second speaker just said, to the satisfaction of the second speaker.

Share what you may have learned about yourself as a listener with your partner. To check your listening accuracy, the two of you may find yourselves later saying to each other: "Do you mean that . . . ?" or "You're saying that. . . ."

> When I am new in a group, I . . .
> When I am feeling anxious in a new situation, I usually . . .
> (Listening check:) "You're saying that . . ."
> The thing that turns me on most is . . .
> Right now I'm feeling . . . (Look your partner in the eye while you respond to this item.)
> When I am rejected, I usually . . .
> The thing that turns me off the most is . . .

[11] Peter G. Banikiotes, J. A. Kubinski, and Sandra A. Pursell, "Sex Role Orientation, Self-disclosure, and Sendee-related Perceptions," *Journal of Counseling Psychology* 28, (1981): 140–146.

Toward you right now, I feel . . .
When I am alone, I usually . . .
(Listening check:) "Do you mean that . . . ?"
I am rebellious when . . .

Checkup: Have a two- or three-minute discussion about this experience so far. Keep eye contact as much as you can, and try to cover the following points:

How well are you listening?
How open and honest have you been?
How eager are you to continue this interchange?
Do you feel that you are getting to know each other?
(Then continue:)
I love . . .
I feel jealous about . . .
Right now I'm feeling . . .
I am afraid of . . .
The thing I like best about you is . . .
You are . . .
Right now I am responding most to . . .

SELF-DISCLOSURE

Expression of your thoughts, ideas, and feelings follows after your awareness of them. This process might also be called *self-expression* or *self-disclosure*. Self-expression and disclosure are important ways of letting the client know that you are a person and not just a role; however, self-disclosure should be used appropriately and not indiscriminately in the counseling sessions.

It is important not to interpret self-disclosure to mean that you ought to talk about yourself, since the primary focus of the interview is on the client. Thus, genuineness does not mean that you reveal your own experiences and values. It does mean, however, that occasionally it is appropriate and helpful for you to reveal or disclose a particular feeling you may have about the counseling session or about the client. The clue to appropriateness is often determined by the question "Whose needs am I meeting when I disclose this idea or feeling—the client's or mine?" Clearly, the former is the much more appropriate instance of the two.

There are several different kinds of self-disclosure. These include:

1. The counselor's own problems
2. Facts about the counselor's role
3. The counselor's reactions to the client (feedback)
4. The counselor's reactions to the counselor-client relationship

Usually, disclosure in the latter two areas is more productive. Many times counselors are tempted to share their problems and concerns when encountering a client with similar problems. In a few instances, you may do so to reassure clients that their concerns are not catastrophic. But, in most other instances, a role reversal occurs—the counselor is gaining something by this sharing with the client. Some research indicates that the counselor who discloses at a high level may be perceived by the client as having significantly poorer mental health.[12] Thus, self-disclosure about your own problems may limit the client's confidence in you as an effective helper.

Often clients may ask questions concerning information about the counselor: "Are you married?" "Why did you become a counselor?" "Are you in school?" These are common types of questions clients ask in seeking facts about the counselor. In this case, it is usually best just to give a direct, brief answer and then return the interview focus to the client. If, however, this is a common occurrence with the same client, there are other ways of responding. Continual client questioning of this sort often indicates that the client is anxious, feels "on the hot seat," and is attempting to get off it by turning the focus onto you. There are better ways to handle this than by spending the interview disclosing facts about yourself! Alternative ways of responding include:

1. Reflecting upon the client's feelings of anxiety:
   "You seem anxious about talking about yourself now."
2. Reflecting upon the process:
   "You seem to be asking a lot of questions now."
3. Making a statement about what you see happening:
   "I think you feel as if you'd been on the 'hot seat' and asking me questions is a good way for you to get off it."

EXERCISE: SELF-DISCLOSURE

Think about yourself in the following instances:

1. You have a client who describes herself as "shy and retiring." During the third interview she says, "I'd like to be like you—you seem so outgoing and comfortable with people. Why don't you just tell me how you got that way?" Do you consider it appropriate then to share some of your experiences with her?
2. You have had one particular client for about seven individual sessions. After the first session, the client has been at least several minutes late for each session and waits until almost the end of the interview to bring up something important to discuss. You feel that he is infringing upon your time. This is preventing you from giving your full attention and understanding to the client. You have acknowledged to yourself that this is bothering you. Is it appropriate then to go ahead and express this to him?

[12] R. G. Weigel et al., "Perceived Self-Disclosure, Mental Health, and Who Is Liked in Group Treatment," *Journal of Counseling Psychology* 19 (1972): 47–52.

Take a few minutes to think about yourself as the counselor in these two examples. Now write in the space below what you would do in each example to communicate "facilitative genuineness."

_____

_____

_____

_____

There are no "correct" answers to these two examples; each counseling interaction is somewhat different. Ultimately, you as the counselor will have to make a decision like this for yourself in each instance. Based on the preceding written material, perhaps you did indicate that it would be more appropriate to express your irritation (the second example) than to disclose your experiences (the first). In the first instance, rather than sharing facts about yourself, there are more productive ways of helping that client reach her goals. For instance, she would be more involved if you suggest role reversal. You become the client; have her be the "outgoing and comfortable" counselor she sees. In the second instance the client is not fulfilling his share of the responsibility by being late; or he is indirectly communicating resistance that needs to be shared and discussed.

Some counselors are able to acknowledge their feelings and determine when these can best be expressed in the interview, but are not sure how to express these kinds of thoughts and feelings to the client. Self-disclosure or expressions of genuineness are often characterized by sharing and feedback statements—statements that convey to the client your sense of what is going on and your feelings about it.[13] These kinds of statements are illustrated by the following examples:

> "I am glad you shared that with me."
> "If that happened to me, I think I'd feel pretty angry."
> "I don't feel that we're getting anywhere right now."

Other examples of sharing kinds of responses are:

> _Client_: "It's hard for me to say so but I really do get a lot out of these sessions."
> _Counselor_: "That makes me feel good to hear you say that."
>   or:
>   "I'm glad to know you feel that way."

Note that in the counselor's sharing statements, the communication is _direct_—it focuses on the counselor's feeling and on the client. It is a better statement than a generalized comment like "I hope most clients would feel the same way." Sharing and feedback statements should avoid the

[13] A. E. Ivey with Lynn Simek-Downing, _Counseling and Psychotherapy: Skills, Theories, and Practice_ (Englewood Cliffs, N.J.: Prentice-Hall, 1980), pp. 103–5.

trap of "counselor language." To begin a sharing and/or feedback state-ment with "I hear you saying," "It seems that you feel," or "I feel that you feel" gets wordy, repetitive, and even phony. Say *exactly* what you mean.

EXERCISE: EXPRESSING COUNSELOR FEELINGS

Sharing and feedback communicate to the client that you have heard or seen something going on, and that you have certain thoughts or feelings about it that you want to communicate. Sometimes you will want to say not only what you feel about a specific instance or experience, but also how you feel about the client. This will be more effective if your feelings are expressed as immediate ones; that is, expressed in the *present* rather than in the past or future. This is the meaning of keeping the process of relationship in the "here and now," using what is going on from moment to moment in each session to build the relationship. It is represented by the type of statement that communicates, "Right now I'm feeling . . ." or "Right now we are. . . ."

To experience this here-and-now kind of communication, try to get in touch with yourself this instant. What are you feeling *this very moment* as you are reading and thinking about this page, this paragraph, this sen-tence? Write, in the space provided, four or five adjectives that express your present feelings. Tune into your nonverbal cues as well (body position, rate of breathing, tension spots, etc.)

_____

_____

_____

EXERCISE: USING SHARING STATEMENTS

With a partner, engage in some sharing-type statements that are direct, specific, and immediate. Can you tune into your feelings as you engage in this kind of communication? What does it do for you and what effect does it have on the other person? Jot down some of these reactions in the space provided. List the sharing statements you have made to your partner.

_____

_____

_____

_____

_____

Sharing statements reflect the expression of the counselor's thoughts and feelings. Feedback statements incorporate a description of *client behavior* as well. Some examples of counselors' feedback-type statements are "When you are continually late to the sessions (client behavior) I feel it is a loss to both of us" (counselor feeling); or, "When you talk about school, your face really lights up" (client behavior), and "It feels good to me to see you so happy about that" (counselor reaction).

You probably are aware as you read that these examples have several characteristics fundamental to effective feedback processes. Such statements express a feeling acknowledged and *owned* by the counselor, as in "when something happens, I feel thus and so," or "when I see you _____, I think _____." They avoid judgment and evaluation. Most of all, they do not accuse or blame, as in the following statement: "You are a real problem to work with because you are always late." In other words, they preserve the dignity and self-respect of the other person involved in the relationship. Furthermore, an effective feedback statement does not contain advice; it is not a "parenting" or scolding statement. It also should concern a behavior or attitude the other person has the capacity to change or modify. It would not be helpful, for instance, to use the following kind of feedback statement: "I just don't like the way you look. Why don't you do something about your complexion?"

Feedback is usually more effective when solicited. Thus, feedback statements that relate to clients' goals or to aspects of the counseling relationship may be better received by clients because of their involvement in this. In any case, though, you can determine the effects of your feedback by the clients' reactions. If your clients are defensive, give detailed explanation or justification, or make strong denials, this is a clue that your feedback was not solicited and that perhaps you have touched on an issue too soon. At this point, clients need an indication of your support and acceptance.

EXERCISE: USING FEEDBACK STATEMENTS

With a partner, try some feedback-type statements that meet the characteristics described in the preceding section. Be sure your responses include a description of your partner's behavior as well as your reactions to it. For example, you might say something like "I appreciate (your feeling) your taking the time to talk with me (partner's behavior)."

List the feedback statements you make to your partner. What are the effects on you? on the other person? on the relationship?

_____

_____

_____

_____

_____

INTENTIONALITY

Finally, we return to the concept of intentionality. There are many references in the literature to "desirable outcomes" for counseling. Ivey and Simek-Downing propose that an appropriate outcome underlying most approaches to counseling is intentionality. They define the intentional person as:

> The person who. . . has a sense of capability. He or she can generate alternative behaviors in a given situation and "approach" a problem from different vantage points. The intentional, fully functioning individual is not bound to one course of action but can respond in the moment to changing life situations and look forward to longer-term goals.[14]

How does this counseling goal affect you? Ivey and Simek-Downing suggest that it is as important for the counselor to be an intentional person as it is for the client. The implication is that the fully functioning counselor is one who can function with alternative behaviors, and can conceptualize from different vantage points. In short, the intentional counselor brings a repertoire of counseling skills and strategies to the counseling session and can operate with a broad range of theoretical explanations of human behavior.

In the chapters to follow, we shall review the essential skills of helping, with the view that they may be rehearsed, integrated, and implemented in future counseling sessions. At the same time, you are encouraged to study, informally or in a formal course, those counseling theories that have proven helpful.

SUMMARY

Although the counseling relationship has some marked differences from other interpersonal relationships, it does serve as a model that the client can use to improve the quality of relationships outside the counseling room. You must assume responsibility at the outset of counseling for those qualities that generate and maintain the relationship process. Later, as the client's comfort and social skills get stronger, the relationship becomes a mutually responsible condition.

Clearly, the counseling relationship cannot succeed without the presence of accurate empathy or understanding of the client's world. When you assume that you understand, but you do not, you and your client detour from a constructive and helpful course and risk the dangers of false conclusions and failure. In a similar manner, if you do not value your client or if you do not consider the client's problems and concerns to be real, you are denying the most reliable information about your client's perceptions. Lacking this information, you cannot help your client develop

[14] Ibid., p. 8.

in more constructive directions. Finally, and underlying both accurate empathy and positive regard, the degree to which you can be honestly and consistently yourself, knowing yourself, sharing yourself with your client will establish the ultimate parameters of the helping relationship.

Although the behaviors presented in this chapter can be learned and incorporated into your style and repertoire, there is a dimension yet to be acknowledged. The integral human element of the counseling relationship cannot exist by mechanical manipulation of certain behaviors at given moments. Your relationship with each client contains its own uniqueness and spontaneity that cannot, without the loss of both genuineness and sincerity, be systematically controlled prior to its occurrence. Your spontaneity, however, will increase rather than decrease, once you have become comfortable with a variety of counseling techniques. While you are learning counselor responses, this ease may not be quite as apparent because you will need to "overlearn" them. However, once the responses suggested in this book have become second nature to you, your spontaneity as a counselor will begin to emerge. You will be on your way to becoming the helper you hope to be.

DISCUSSION QUESTIONS

1. How do you approach a new relationship? What conditions do you require to be met before you open yourself to a closer relationship?
2. What were the "unwritten rules" in your family about interactions with nonfamily members?
3. If you were a client, what conditions would you look for in your counselor?

RECOMMENDED READINGS?

BOY, ANGELO V., and GERALD J. PINE,   *Client-Centered Counseling: A Renewal*. Boston: Allyn & Bacon, 1982.

The authors bring a concise and readable update of the practice of client-centered counseling to the counselor trainee. Their chapter on the counseling relationship is particularly recommended.

BOZARTH, JEROLD D., "Beyond Reflection: Emergent Modes of Empathy." In *Client-Centered Therapy and the Person-Centered Approach*, ed. Ronald F. Levant and John M. Shlien. pp 59–75. New York: Praeger, 1984.

Bozarth examines current thinking and misinterpretations of what constitutes "therapeutic empathy." Through examples, he illustrates how empathy and reflection are different concepts. This chapter is an excellent summary on the subject of empathy.

CORMIER, L. SHERILYN, and HAROLD L. HACKNEY. *The Professional Counselor: A Process Guide to Helping*. Englewood Cliffs, N.J.: Prentice-Hall, 1987.

Rapport and relationship (Chapter 3) are considered as part of a five-stage process for therapeutic change in counseling.

HANSEN, JAMES C., RICHARD R. STEVIC, and RICHARD W. WARNER, JR.,   *Counseling: Theory and Process.* Boston: Allyn & Bacon, 1986.

Chapter 12, "Counseling as a Relationship," provides the reader with an in-depth examination of the therapeutic relationship, its component parts, and its assumptions.

LIETAER, GERMAIN,   "Unconditional Positive Regard: A Controversial Basic Attitude in Client-Centered Therapy." In *Client-Centered Therapy and the Person-Centered Approach*, ed. Ronald F. Levant and John M. Shlien, pp. 41–58. New York: Praeger, 1984.

The author provides an in-depth examination of the implications of both positive regard and unconditionality and how they impact upon the counseling process.

CHAPTER THREE

Attending to Clients

Thus far we have identified several conditions that affect the development of the counseling relationship. Those conditions—accurate empathy, positive regard, and genuineness or congruence—are called *core conditions* because they are central to the therapeutic process. While these core conditions are necessary, the counselor must also bring other skills and knowledge to the therapeutic process. Certainly the first of these skills is the ability to *listen* actively and attentively to the client. This objective is not so simple as it might appear. It involves more than the attentive ear.

Have you ever talked to someone who was fiddling with a pencil, staring around the room, or who seemed otherwise distracted as he or she listened to you? If you have—and who hasn't—you will recall how this felt. The listener may have heard all that you said, but you probably interpreted his or her behavior as a lack of interest, concentration, or present-centeredness. And, if that seemed to be the case, you may have found it difficult to continue the conversation. Clients exhibit this same sensitivity to whether the counselor is paying attention to what they say. Counseling research strongly suggests that nonverbal behavior does influence the verbal message with which it is paired, particularly when inconsistencies exist between verbal and nonverbal messages.[1]

This chapter is concerned with the behaviors that do or do not facilitate communication and the core conditions in counseling. In addition, attending skills used by the counselor to assure the client and to support or reinforce the client are examined. These skills are very important for the client who is feeling vulnerable, uncertain, nonconfident, or nontrusting.

[1] Judy A. Tyson and Shavaun M. Wall, "Effect of Inconsistency between Counselor Verbal and Nonverbal Behavior on Perceptions of Counselor Attributes," *Journal of Counseling Psychology* 30, no. 3 (1983): 433–37.

One precondition for the existence of these reinforcing or supporting behaviors is an awareness of the client's communication. This awareness must then be communicated through your undistracted attentiveness to the client. Attentiveness is one way of saying, "I am following both your message and your metacommunication; I am experiencing as you are experiencing this moment; I am invested and involved in your story." Studies have indicated that attentiveness is related to other counselor attitudes, most notably empathy and involvement. Counselor interest and commitment appear to be related to clients' and observers' perceptions of the counselor's empathy.[2] Attentiveness, empathy, and affectional nurturance all appear to be related to one another.[3] Furthermore, subtle reinforcers, such as interest and approval, however they are expressed, have more far-reaching effect than do overt reactions such as "That's good."

COMMUNICATION OF ATTENTIVENESS

Attentiveness is communicated primarily through three channels: facial expressions, bodily positions and movement, and verbal response.[4] These communication modes offer cues to the client about the level of acceptance, approval, agreement, rejection, or indifference associated with the reinforcing behavior.[5] The meanings we attach to different gestures or words have been learned. Some of the meanings are fairly standardized, and others have distinct regional or cultural variances. For example, do you prefer to have people look at you when you talk to them? Most Americans do, but some American Indians do not, and studies suggest that some inner-city American black youths do not. When you are telling someone what you think, what would be your reaction if that person began to frown? If the frown was not consistent with your feelings, you probably would begin to question the inconsistency between your message and the listener's response. If you feel strongly about a topic and the other person does not seem to care about it, are you likely to continue telling the person about your feelings? No, since most of us want to know that our feelings are falling upon sympathetic ears.

For these and many more reasons, your behavior can contribute to your client's feelings of security. This increased sense of security that occurs at the same time clients are talking about themselves can become a self-reinforcing phenomenon. We have all had the experience of entering a new activity and feeling nervous and unsure of ourselves. But as we stayed with the activity and nothing bad (perhaps even some good things) happened, before long, our self-confidence began to grow. So it is with counsel-

[2] P. F. Caracena and J. R. Vicory, "Correlates of Phenomenological and Judged Empathy," *Journal of Counseling Psychology* 16 (1969): 510–15.

[3] Harold L. Hackney, A. E. Ivey, and E. R. Oetting, "Attending, Island, and Hiatus Behavior: A Process Conception of Counselor and Client Interaction," *Journal of Counseling Psychology* 17 (1970): 342–46.

[4] A. E. Ivey, *Microcounseling: Innovations in Interviewing Training* (Springfield, Ill.: Charles C. Thomas, 1971), p. 41.

[5] Hackney, Ivey, and Oetting, "Attending, Island, and Hiatus Behavior," pp. 342–46.

ing. As the client begins to experience your acceptance, your understanding, and your commitment, the feelings of vulnerability, uncertainty, caution, or lack of trust begin to dissipate. Is this a predictable reaction? Yet, it is, with the majority of clients who are in search of themselves, a better way to live life, or a better way to relate to others.

FACIAL EXPRESSIONS

Knapp has observed that the face is the "primary site for communication of emotional states; it reflects interpersonal attitudes; it provides nonverbal feedback on the comments of others; and some say it is the primary source of information next to human speech."[6] Your facial expressions communicate messages to the client that are as meaningful as those you receive from the client's facial expressions. A primary, though often not intentional, way that counselors use their facial expressions is to reinforce client behavior. Perhaps it would be more accurate to say that the effect of your facial expressions is to reinforce, either positively or negatively, clients' verbal behavior. These facial gestures are primarily of three types: eye contact, head nods, and manipulation of facial muscles to produce smiles, frowns, quizzical looks, indifference, and so forth. We shall consider the effects of each of these separately.

Eye Contact

What is the effect of eye contact? Research into interpersonal interaction indicates more than one effect. Knapp observes that eye contact "is frequently indicative of the nature of the relationship between the interactants."[7] It may signal a need for affiliation, involvement, or inclusion; it may reflect the quality of an existing relationship; or it may enhance the communication of a complex message. Eye contact can also produce anxiety in the other person. A gaze lasting longer than about ten seconds can signal aggressiveness rather than acceptance.[8]

Good eye contact, eye contact that reinforces clients and makes their communication easier, lies somewhere between the fixed gaze and "shifty eyes," or frequent breaks of eye contact. Look at clients when they are talking. Occasionally, permit your eyes to drift to an object away, *but not far away*, from the client. Then return your eyes to the client. Let yourself be natural. Do not be afraid to invite the client into the world of your vision.

EXERCISE: EYE CONTACT

Perhaps you can better grasp the effects of eye contact by participating in the following dyadic exercise. One of you should be the talker and the

[6] Mark L. Knapp, *Nonverbal Communication in Human Interaction*, 2d ed. (New York: Holt, Rinehart & Winston, 1978), p. 263.

[7] Ibid., p. 132.

[8] H. T. Moore and A. R. Gilliand, "The Measure of Aggressiveness," *Journal of Applied Psychology* 5 (1921): 101–2.

other the listener. While the talker speaks, the listener should listen, but avoid eye contact with the speaker. Then, discuss the following questions: What are the effects on the speaker? How well did the speaker feel that he or she was able to communicate? Try the exercise again, but this time, maintain eye contact with the speaker as described in the previous section. What effect does this have? Reverse roles and repeat the exercise.

The Head Nod

The affirmative head nod also indicates to clients that you are listening and being attentive. When overdone, however, it can become distracting. You do want clients to be aware of your attentiveness. The use of occasional head nods, paired with good eye contact, will reassure clients of your involvement and commitment.

Animation

Animation in facial expression gives clients the feeling that you are alert and responding to ongoing communication. It may be that your facial expressions serve as a mirror for clients' feelings as well as an acceptance of them. Certainly, an absence of facial expressions (the proverbial dead-pan) will suggest a lack of interest, awareness, or mental presence to clients. The most noticeable expression is the smile. The appropriate use of smiles can have a powerful effect upon clients, particularly when paired with occasional head nods.[9] But continuous smiling becomes a negative stimulus. Frequent frowns can communicate disapproval. Occasional frowns, on the other hand, communicate your failure to follow or understand a particular point, and are therefore useful.

EXERCISE: FACIAL EXPRESSIONS

With a partner, designate one of you as speaker and the other as the listener. While the speaker shares one of his or her concerns, the listener's task is:

1. Do not respond with *any* facial expression or animation whatsoever while the speaker is talking; maintain complete facial passivity.
2. After two or three minutes, respond with a facial reaction that is opposite of the feelings and concerns being expressed by the speaker. For example, if the speaker is talking seriously, smile and look happy.
3. After another three minutes or so, respond with facial animation and expression that mirror the kind and intensity of feelings being expressed by the speaker.

Discuss the different results produced by these three approaches. Reverse roles and repeat the exercise. What can you conclude about facial attentive-

[9] Harold L. Hackney, "Facial Gestures and Subject Expression of Feeling," *Journal of Counseling Psychology* 21 (1974): 163–78.

ness as a result of this exercise? What have you learned about yourself and your facial gestures? What do you want to change about your facial gestures and how do you intend to bring this change about?

BODY MESSAGES

The key to body communication is the amount of tension that you are feeling. A relaxed body posture indicates comfort, both with the counseling setting and with the topic being discussed. Body tension communicates action. It may reflect a "working" moment for you, involvement with the client, movement toward a goal, or preparation for something new. Or it may reflect your discomfort with yourself, with the topic, or with the client. Body tension that is continuous will probably communicate discomfort with the client; selective body tension will indicate discomfort with yourself. In order to manipulate or use body tension as a message, you must begin from a base of relaxation. The following exercise may help you to achieve a desired state of relaxation.

EXERCISE: RELAXING

While sitting down, raise your hand and arms three to four inches above the armrests of the chair, and then let them drop. Feel the tension flow out of your arms. Repeat this and try to increase the relaxation. Let your back and buttocks be in contact with as much of the chair as possible. Feel the chair pressing against your body. Tense the muscles in your legs and then release the tension. Feel the surge of warmth in your muscles as your legs relax. Repeat this tensing and releasing of leg muscles several times, each time achieving a little more relaxation. Now take three or four deep breaths slowly. After each breath, slowly release the air from your lungs. Do you feel more relaxed than when you started?

Do this exercise again, this time without any interruptions between different body exercises. This is a good exercise to do just before seeing a client. It is one of the ways by which you can prepare yourself for the session. As you do the exercise more often, you will find it easier and quicker to achieve a surprisingly comfortable state of relaxation.

Together facial expressions and body messages constitute the counselor's visible behavior. The impact of visible behavior on communication is considerable, as the following exercise will prove.

EXERCISE: THE IMPACT OF VISIBLE BEHAVIOR

Egan has described a simple exercise that illustrates the importance of what we see in another person when we communicate.[10] This exercise

---

[10] Gerard Egan, *Interpersonal Living: A Skills/Contract Approach to Human Relations Training in Groups* (Monterey, Calif.: Brooks/Cole, 1976), p. 101.

will give you an opportunity to measure the effect of your facial and body gestures on the person receiving your message. Select as your partner a person you have been wanting to involve in a conversation. Sit down facing each other. Each of you close your eyes and keep them closed throughout the conversation. Talk to each other for about five minutes. Then open your eyes, complete the conversation, and discuss the differences between visual and nonvisual communication. What compensations did you have to make while talking without sight? How successful did you believe you were in your communication attempts? What, in particular, were you missing in terms of visual feedback from your partner?

VERBAL BEHAVIOR

The things you say will have immediate impact upon clients. Many studies have shown that the counselor's responses can mold and shape the direction of the client's responses. There are several points to be considered in terms of your verbal impact. First, fit your comments or questions into the context of the topic at hand. Don't interrupt clients or jump topics. Stay with the topics that clients introduce and help them develop and pursue them. This implies more than a technique; it is a highly conscious awareness of what is going on between you and your client. Practice verbal following in the following exercise.

EXERCISE: VERBAL FOLLOWING

In the roles of counselor/client, choose a partner and sit in pairs. Concentrate on using the verbal reinforcing behaviors discussed in this chapter. In your responses, react only to what the client has just said; do not add a new idea. Let your thinking be as close as possible to that of the client.

Prevent your facial gestures, body gestures, and verbal responses from distracting the client. After five minutes, stop the exercise and discuss with your client: What was your client most aware of in your behavior? How well did your client think you were understanding his or her communication? What, if any, behavior got in your client's way? Now reverse roles and repeat the exercise.

Vocal Characteristics

The use of a well-modulated, unexcited vocal tone and pitch will reassure clients of your own comfort with their problems. The use of intermittent one-word phrases (minimal verbal stimuli) serves much the same purpose as do the head nod and eye contact. These are verbal signs that you are listening and following what the client is saying. The more common minimal verbal stimuli are "mm-hmm," "mmm," "ah," and so forth. There is one hazard that should be mentioned: Overuse of these vocal stimuli can produce a "parrotlike" effect that has negative results. Later chapters will describe how you can use minimal verbal stimuli and other types of reinforcing behaviors to assist clients in developing their thinking.

SUMMARY

In summary, one of the major goals in the counseling setting is to listen attentively and to communicate this attentiveness through the use of eye contact, intermittent head nods, a variety of facial expressions, relaxed posture, modulated voice, minimal verbal stimuli, and verbal components that follow the client's topics. The effect of this communication will be to reinforce verbal behavior, comfort, and clients' potential to examine and understand themselves.

DISCUSSION QUESTIONS

1. How much do you rely upon reactions (gestures, verbal responses) from the other person when you are trying to communicate an important message?
2. What is your typical response when you feel that you are failing in your attempt to communicate with another person?
3. What goals or objectives have you set for yourself in terms of improving your ability to be a good listener? What do you plan to do to achieve these goals?

RECOMMENDED READINGS

EGAN, GERARD, *Interpersonal Living: A Skills/Contract Approach to Human Relations Training in Groups*. Monterey, Calif.: Brooks/Cole, 1986.

Although this book is addressed to people working in groups, the skills are easily applied to the one-to-one setting. Part 3, in particular, is outstanding, covering topics like "Attending and Listening"; "The Communication of Accurate Empathic Understanding: Creating a Climate of Support"; and "Genuineness and Respect as Communication Skills."

EKMAN, PAUL, *Emotion in the Human Face*, 2d ed. New York: Cambridge University Press, 1982.

This book presents an excellent review of the research and conclusions related to the facial expression of human emotion. While it is not specifically directed to the counselor, counselors should find it informative and useful in their work.

HACKNEY, HAROLD L., "The Evolution of Empathy," *Personnel and Guidance Journal* 57 (1978): 35–38.

This article examines how the empathy construct has evolved in meaning from its earliest usage to present training practices. Distinctions between the condition and how it is communicated are noted with the suggestion that practicing counselors should reexamine the original concept.

HACKNEY, HAROLD L., A. E. IVEY, and E. R. OETTING,   "Attending, Island, and Hiatus Behavior: A Process Conception of Counselor and Client Interaction," *Journal of Counseling Psychology* 17 (July 1970): 342–46.

The authors discuss how counselor-attending behavior, verbal and nonverbal, affects and reinforces the kinds of topics the client discusses.

KNAPP, MARK L.,   *Nonverbal Communication in Human Interaction*, 2d ed. New York: Holt, Rinehart & Winston, 1978.

Three chapters in this book are particularly relevant to the counselor: Chapter 4, "Effects of Physical Behavior on Human Communication"; Chapter 5, "Effects of the Face and Eyes on Human Communication"; and Chapter 6, "Effects of Vocal Cues Which Accompany Spoken Words." Knapp has written a highly readable and interesting book that reflects research and its implications for communication.

CHAPTER FOUR

Recognizing Communication Patterns

We have shown how verbal and nonverbal behaviors are the means by which core conditions such as empathy and warmth are communicated. The next level in this very complicated process involves the communication patterns that emerge as the relationship develops. We have already alluded to communication patterns (Chapter 2) in Boy and Pine's description of the reciprocal nature of the counselor-client relationship.[1] While their perspective is that of person-centered therapy, the same process may be described using the social-influence perspective.[2] Issues related to the locus of control and responsibility in the session, choice of topics, timing, and other therapeutic logistics are undefined at the outset of counseling. In the first few sessions, these issues are resolved, either openly or tacitly, and become apparent through understanding of the communication patterns that evolve.

There are many ways to think about patterning in the counseling process. Some patterning takes the form of ritual, while other patterning is responsive. That is to say, some of the behaviors become ritualized as a function of routine; for example, the client always chooses the chair facing the window, the counselor always begins by asking, "What is on your mind today?" and so forth. Other patterns are negotiations between counselor and client, the intent of which may be to settle such matters as, "Are we really going to work today?" or "I want you to take charge because I'm feeling overwhelmed." An example of this has been provided in a study by Friedlander and Phillips, who found that frequent topic shifts (or changes) in the early sessions were an indication that a struggle for control

[1] Angelo V. Boy and Gerald J. Pine, *Client-Centered Counseling: A Renewal* (Boston: Allyn & Bacon, 1982).

[2] N. M. Meara, H. B. Pepinsky, J. W. Shannon, and W. A. Murray, "A Comparison of Semantic Communication in and Expectations for Counseling across Three Theoretical Orientations," *Journal of Counseling Psychology* 28 (1981): 110–18.

over the process was being waged between counselor and client.[3] If such a struggle was going on and the counselor was unaware of it, the implications for progress would be questionable.

RITUALIZED PATTERNS OF COMMUNICATION

Ritualized patterns may be either situation-specific or idiosyncratic to the individuals involved. We have already mentioned examples of situation-specific patterning with the client who always chooses a certain chair to sit in. This "fact" of repeated choice may arise out of a very simple condition. It was the chair selected by the client at the initial session, and its continued selection in subsequent sessions both offers familiar ground and reflects that the client feels no need to make a different choice. But if, in the fifth session, the client arrives and, with no explanation, chooses a different chair, the act of choice may contain unspecified meaning. In other words, through the act of choosing, something is communicated, but what is communicated is unclear until the counselor questions the client.

Ritualized Counselor Patterns

The same situation may apply to the counselor. Most experienced counselors develop a "style" of interaction with their clients. While their style takes individuals into account, it is nonetheless patterned and, as such, is a kind of trademark of that counselor's work. For example, a counselor may use the first five to ten minutes of the session as relationship time and may communicate this to clients. Or a different counselor may view the first few minutes as "history-taking" time. However, should a client arrive in a distraught state, that pattern may be suspended and therapeutic work may begin immediately.

Ritualized Client Patterns

Clients also become involved in ritualized patterns of communication. Often these patterns evolve out of assumptions about what the counselor wants or expects from the client. For example, a client may assume that the counselor expects to hear an account of the week's worries. The fact that this happened in the second session has led the client to think such an account is expected, and so he continues the practice in subsequent sessions. Thus, although the activity has little or nothing to do with the process, it remains a part of the pattern.

INTERACTIVE COMMUNICATION PATTERNS

Most patterning, and certainly the most significant patterning that occurs in the counseling session is interactive in nature. It has been suggested

[3] Myrna L. Friedlander and Susan D. Phillips, "Stochastic Process Analysis of Interactive Discourse in Early Counseling Interviews," *Journal of Counseling Psychology* 31 (1984): 139–48.

by Cormier and Hackney that most clients approach counseling with two conflicting motivations: (1) "I know I need help"; and (2) "I wish I weren't here."[4] Given this dual set of motivations, the client may be expected to convey conflicting and even contradictory communications at times. Similarly, counselors must resolve the potential conflict that was mentioned in Chapter 2 regarding unconditional positive regard and congruence.[5] We mention these conflicting tendencies because they can confuse the communication process. It is essential that the counselor know his or her inner motivations and conflicts. In addition to these inner motivations, there are more obvious and more common social interaction patterns that beginning counselors must consider.

Interactive Counselor Patterns

There are basically three kinds of communication patterns common in ordinary social intercourse but inappropriate for the counselor. These may be identified as (1) underparticipation, (2) overparticipation, and (3) distracting participation.

The counselor who is an underparticipant may have a fear of involvement, either with the client or with a certain problem area. The underparticipatory counselor's verbal communication is not direct; there is often too much reliance on the nonverbal. The underparticipatory counselor may convey to the client that he or she is not able or willing to help him, thus reducing the client's faith in the counselor and in the counseling process. Behaviorally, an underparticipatory counselor can be described as follows:

NONVERBAL CHARACTERISTICS

1. May appear stiff; little body movement.
2. Body position often pulled away from the client.
3. Eyes are often averted and downcast.
4. Sometimes evidence of stooped shoulders, shrugging of shoulders.

VERBAL CHARACTERISTICS

1. Verbal speech is characterized by monosyllabic responses or phrases, rather than by complete sentences.
2. Verbal speech often is not continuous.
3. Sometimes evidence of self-deprecating statements.
4. Verbal responses are primarily reflective in nature.

---

[4] L. Sherilyn Cormier and Harold Hackney, *The Professional Counselor: A Process Guide to Helping* (Englewood Cliffs, N.J.: Prentice-Hall, 1987), p. 20.

[5] Germain Lietaer, "Unconditional Positive Regard: A Controversial Basic Attitude in Client-Centered Therapy," Chapter 3 in *Client-Centered Therapy and the Person-Centered Approach: New Directions in Theory, Research, and Practice*, ed. Ronald F. Levant and John M. Schlien (New York: Praeger, 1984).

PARALANGUAGE CHARACTERISTICS

   1. Tone of voice is soft and weak; responses sometimes trail off into silence.

   The counselor who is an overparticipant may use this response style as a way to cover up feelings of anxiety in the interview. Exerting control is often used as an anxiety-reduction tool. This counselor relies heavily on action-oriented, confrontative statements and jumps to conclusions without much awareness of the client's feelings. Behaviorally, an overparticipatory counselor can be characterized as follows:

NONVERBAL CHARACTERISTICS

   1. Often a great deal of body movement; many gestures, fidgeting.
   2. Much animation and expression, often to the point of being distracting.

VERBAL CHARACTERISTICS

   1. Verbal speech is characterized by a high output of words, often a compulsive flow of verbiage.
   2. Verbal speech is often laden with detail and repetition.
   3. Length of response frequently exceeds length of preceding client response.

PARALANGUAGE CHARACTERISTICS

   1. Rate of verbal speech is quite fast; pauses between sentences are few.
   2. Tone of voice is often high and loud.

   There is another kind of communication pattern exhibited by some counselors that is inappropriate for the counseling setting. This involves a distracting kind of participation in the interview. The counselor may be involved, but has difficulty focusing on the client and responding to the primary stimuli emitted by the client. The counselor who is a distracting participant frequently responds to secondary and irrelevant aspects of the client's communication. Behaviorally, this kind of inappropriate participation can be described as follows:

NONVERBAL CHARACTERISTICS

   1. Inappropriate smiling, frequent nervous laughter.

VERBAL CHARACTERISTICS

   1. Speech is characterized by distractors; speaker does not respond to the stimulus at hand, but to a secondary stimulus.
   2. Speech is further characterized by shifts in topics.
   3. Speech often centers on others rather than on the client, and on the past rather than the present.

EXERCISE: ANALYZING COUNSELOR RESPONSES

Below are some client statements followed by counselor responses. Describe each counselor response: Do you feel that it is a response to the client's statement? If not, describe the nature of the inappropriate response, such as *shift of topic, focus on others*, or *focus on past*.

Client A: "I think I just have to go away for awhile. The pressure is really building up."

Counselor: "What would Bob say to that?"

The counselor did/did not (circle one) respond to the client's statement. If the counselor did not respond to the client's statement, the nature of the inappropriate response was _____.

Client B: "She doesn't really care anymore, and I've got to learn to accept that."

Counselor: "You are fairly sure that she doesn't care."

The counselor did/did not (circle one) respond to the client's statement. If the counselor did not respond to the client's statement, the nature of the inappropriate response was _____.

Client C: "Money is the biggest problem I have in school. The grades aren't that hard to get."

Counselor: "What did you do last year?"

The counselor did/did not (circle one) respond to the client's statement. If the counselor did not respond to the client's statement, the nature of the inappropriate response was _____.

Client D: "The job I have isn't fun, but I'm afraid if I quit, I might not get another job."

Counselor: "Jobs are really getting hard to find."

The counselor did/did not (circle one) respond to the client's statement. If the counselor did not respond to the client's statement, the nature of the inappropriate response was _____.

These exchanges illustrate some of the common pitfalls that await the counselor. In the exchange with client A, the response was probably inappropriate. The counselor seems to have topic-jumped by bringing up Bob. In addition, the counselor ignored the client's reference to the pressure and its effect upon him. The response given to client B could be quite appropriate, though it isn't the only possible appropriate response. The counselor is responding directly to what the client said. The inappropriateness of the response to client C is more obvious, though no one would be surprised to hear the response if it were a social setting rather than a counseling setting. The counselor really didn't respond to any of the key ideas in the client's statement (money, problem, or grades). Instead, the counselor decided, for some reason, to collect information about the client. Finally, the response to client D is also inappropriate. The client is talking about feelings ("isn't fun"; "afraid"). The counselor's response has nothing to do with the client. Instead, the counselor shifted the focus to a social commentary on the current economic scene.

Now that you are aware of behavioral descriptions of inappropriate social behaviors and communication patterns in the counseling setting, can you deduce some appropriate behaviors? Be specific as to nonverbal components (face, eyes, tone of voice, rate of speech, etc.), body-language components (head, arms, body position, etc.), and verbal components (choice of words, types of responses, etc.). List them on a sheet of paper.

Discuss what you specified as appropriate counselor behaviors and communication patterns. Try some out. You may find that you will need to eliminate some behaviors and relearn some others. This will take a little time and practice until you feel completely comfortable with your new styles. With a partner, decide which of the following appropriate counselor behaviors are not present in your current repertoire:

Facial animation
Good eye contact
Occasional head nodding
Soft, firm tone of voice
Occasional smiling
Occasional gesturing with hands
Moderate rate of speech
Response to primary stimulus of client communication
Verbal speech centers on client and on immediate present
Occasional use of minimal verbal reinforcers (e.g., "mm-hmm")

Set behavioral goals for yourself. What is it that you would like to be able to do as a result of your newly acquired learnings? Share this with your partner. Make some commitment about the kinds of things you are going to do this week to implement your goals. Your partner should do the same thing. This way you and your partner can give each other feedback about goal attainment as you continue to interact.

SILENCE

For most beginning counselors, silence can be frightening. It seems to bring the total focus of attention upon them, revealing their most glaring weaknesses as counselors. At least, this is how many beginning counselors describe their experiences with silence. As a result, their tendency is to say something—anything—to prevent silence. Typically, a question is asked. It is often a bad question, one that can be answered by a minimal response from the client. The answer to the question is relatively unimportant, since the question was not well thought out by the counselor. The counselor may not even be listening to the answer. Such a state of affairs suggests that it is the counselor's responsibility to keep the client talking, that talking is the only evidence that the client is working, and that silence is probably nontherapeutic, a waste of time. None of these assumptions is valid.

Silence has a similar effect upon clients. They also perceive silence as a demanding condition and feel a need to respond, to fill the gaps of silence with talking. Because clients react to silence in this way, you can use silence as a counseling technique and as a way of responding to clients. Silence has another meaning that is important to acknowledge. After a period of hard work in the session, or after a moment of significant insight, the client often needs time to absorb the experience, to fit it into his or her existing system. This results in an *integration silence*, one in which the client is experiencing fully the therapeutic moment. You may not encounter this in your first counseling sessions, but you will as you gain experience.

Types of Silence

Silence can be a therapeutic moment as well as self-conscious moment. But what makes one silence different from another? What are the dimensions of silence in a counseling session? Silence can be categorized broadly as counselor-induced or client-induced. Counselor-induced silence occurs at a time when the focus of the interview is on the counselor. Said another way, if the counselor, rather than the client, is feeling responsible for the moment and responds with silence, that is a counselor-induced silence. Conversely, if the client has been talking, assuming responsibility, and then stops, that is a client-induced silence.

Counselor-Induced Silence

Counselor-induced silence can be examined in two contexts: the counselor's intentions and the consequences of the silence. Counselor intentions can vary widely. On the one hand, we have the underparticipatory counselor who gives very little verbally. It is a style of behavior that may reflect the counselor's interpersonal interactions with people in general. It does not reflect therapeutic intentions. Rather, it may indicate a generalized tendency to hide, to withhold, to protect oneself from other people.

A second form of silence is that which occurs unsystematically. It is like being "at a loss for words." Its intention is probably to give the counselor time to absorb and comprehend all that is going on at the moment. Again, it is not intended by the counselor to be a therapeutic moment, though the effect is often therapeutic. Many times we have seen a counselor fail to respond to the moment, for personal reasons, and the effect was to encourage the client to continue more deeply into the topic or the feeling. When this happens, the counselor is more apt to feel lucky rather than competent.

The third form of counselor-induced silence is that which the counselor has deliberately presented. It may be that the counselor has been very active and has decided to reduce that activity, thus transferring more responsibility over to the client. Or it may be that the counselor senses a momentum on the client's part that will lead to insight, commitment, or new relevant issues. In this case, the counselor chooses not to respond, in order not to interfere with or impede the client's psychological momentum.

Client-Induced Silence

Client-induced silence also has varied intentions and consequences. As we have noted with counselor silence, client silence is affected by the issue of responsibility and what to do with it. If the client is feeling irresponsible or underresponsible, the intention behind the silence may be antitherapeutic or antigrowth. For example, suppose Betty has developed a life pattern of avoiding some personal issues. When these issues arise, her natural response is to deny or ignore them by deflecting attention from herself. In the counseling setting, she may be aware that these personal issues are the source of her difficulties. Yet her natural reaction continues to be avoidance, deflection, or resistance. In this example, Betty's silence would reflect an attempt to transfer momentary responsibility over to the counselor and away from herself. If she is successful, the consequence would be yet another time when important issues are avoided and underresponsibility is rewarded.

Another reason clients lapse into silence is to try to catch up on the progress of the moment. Counseling sessions sometimes move very quickly, covering a lot of ground, incorporating and relating many issues to one another. There is a need to stop, catch one's breath, observe the progress, or comprehend the implications. This is a very therapeutic type of silence. It allows clients to fit the new growth or insight that has occurred into their existing system. In effect, the client alters the existing system to include what has just been learned. There are also times when client-induced silence results from clients' opening some new doors to their awareness. Robert, who with his wife, Carolyn, had been in counseling for several weeks, lapsed into a silence during a discussion of "families of origin" (a technique used to identify styles, expectations, rules of interpersonal living). After a silence of a minute or more, he stated to the therapist and his wife, "I've been living with Carolyn for six years and thinking that I was overcoming the life I had with my parents. Now I can see that I have been more a reflection of my parents' home than I realized. I wonder what I really do believe in and want from my own family."

How are you to know what kind of silence is occurring? The intention of a client-induced silence must always be inferred. By watching the client closely, by being sensitive to the themes, the issues, and the feelings being expressed, you will be gathering clues to what is happening. Is the client relaxed? Are the client's eyes fixed upon something without being focused? This may mean the client is thinking about or pondering something or examining a new idea, or ruminating around in his or her mind. Or is the client tense, appearing nervous, looking from one object to another and avoiding eye contact? If so, this may mean that he or she is avoiding some topic or idea.

Therapeutic Silence

Skilled counselors often use silence as their best technique for specific situations. This does not suggest that they are inactive. There is always nonverbal behavior that adds meaning to the silence, thus communicating a therapeutic message to the client. We have discussed nonverbal communications in Chapter 4. The messages that the counselor may seek to communicate include "I want us to move a bit more slowly"; "I want you to think more about what you just said"; "I don't accept the message you just presented"; or "I care very much about you and your feelings in this moment." There are other therapeutic messages that can be communicated through silence, but these tend to be the most common.

Pacing the Interview

Counseling interviews can be compared to a musical score. They have variations in theme, timing, activity, and inactivity. As you acquire self-comfort and skills, you will become aware that the different times in an interview have very different qualities. The counselor is a conductor of sorts for this therapeutic score. There are times when the client is hyperactive, babbling, or overacting, and the desired objective is to slow down the pace of the session. You can always verbally call attention to the client's activity; oftentimes silence achieves the same objective. You may not respond with total silence. Occasional verbal responses let the client know that you are still a participant. But you may want to monitor your reactions and not respond to all that stimulates you.

Silent Focusing

One of the ways in which silence is most useful is to focus attention on the moment. It is like stopping to listen to the echo. Throughout the book we will be suggesting ways in which you can help clients hear themselves. Silence is the first of these ways. Sometimes clients make totally irrational statements. By not responding to the statement, you allow the client messages to remain present, to continue to be heard even by the clients themselves. Or clients may make a statement of such relevance that you want to give them time to absorb the impact of that relevance. This would be the case when a client has just acknowledged a significant insight and needs time to fit this insight into an existing system of meanings.

Responding to Defenses

Occasionally, clients come to the interview filled with emotions that belong to other people or situations, yet they spill them out on you or the counseling process. Or you may make a statement to which the client responds defensively. These situations often reflect a lack of client awareness, though they are moments when the potential for awareness is great. The temptation for you may be to give the client insight into the situation. Often it is more meaningful to allow clients to give themselves that insight. This can be done by using silence as your response.

Silent Caring

Silent caring occurs in those moments when no words are an adequate response to the feelings that are present. It may be a moment of quiet weeping for the client. Or it may be a moment of heavy melancholy. Whatever the feeling may be, it is one of those moments when experiencing the feeling fully is more important than making it go away. You can communicate your compassion and involvement very clearly with caring silence.

EXERCISE: BEING COMFORTABLE WITH SILENCE

In our culture, people often have to learn to be silent. Perhaps you find silence to be intense and uncomfortable. If so, this exercise will help you to become more comfortable with silence. Team up with two other people. One person will be the talker, you be the listener, and the third person can be the timekeeper. Invite the talker to talk about anything he or she wishes. You will listen and respond. But, before you respond, allow a pause to occur. Begin with five-second pauses. Gradually increase the duration of pauses until you are allowing fifteen seconds to pass before responding. The timekeeper should sit in a position from which he or she can signal the number of seconds to you without distracting the talker. After a ten-minute discussion, rotate roles and repeat the exercise until all three of you have had a turn as listener.

As a variation on this exercise, consider your contacts with people you encounter every day. Become conscious of your interaction patterns. Do you interject your reactions as soon as the other person has completed a communication? Do you interrupt the other person, thus preventing the slightest possibility of a silence? During the next few days, monitor your response behavior. When someone speaks to you, pause and think about the message for a few seconds and then give your response. Record any feedback you receive from your friends or acquaintances regarding your communication behavior.

SUMMARY

The practice of professional counseling involves a compromise between personal authenticity and professional skills. Both authenticity and skills are maintained by patterns of behavior that emerge as the counselor matures and grows in experience. Similarly, clients evolve patterns of behavior that reflect both their personal qualities and their problems. We have noted how these patterns affect and are affected by the counselor's interventions. The beginning counselor's most noticeable patterns are those involving interactive qualities—underparticipation, overparticipation, or distracting participation. As the counselor's comfort level with the counseling setting improves, these patterns may be examined for their effect upon the session. More subtle, and perhaps of greater concern, are the counselor patterns that become ritualized. Ritualized patterns exist for expediency's sake. They are the behavioral shorthand that allows more efficient functioning. The problem is that efficient functioning may not be effective functioning, particularly in the helping relationship. Consequently, it is professionally imperative that counselors examine their patterns of interaction with clients, not just early in their careers but throughout their careers.

DISCUSSION QUESTIONS

1. What are some additional examples for social behaviors that you would find distracting if you were involved in a sensitive discussion of your private life?

2. Recall an incident in which you were sharing a significant moment with another person and that person displayed some distracting behavior. What was the effect of that person's behavior on you? What did you decide was the reason for that person's behavior?

3. If you are able to eliminate inappropriate social behavior from your counseling repertoire, what impression do you think this will make on your client?

4. What types of messages can be communicated with a silence? How many of these messages might occur in a counseling session? How can you tell one message from another?

RECOMMENDED READINGS

GINOTT, HAIM G.,   *Between Parent and Child*. New York: Avon, 1969.

Although this book is written to and for parents, it is essential reading for the future child counselor. It focuses upon communication between adult and child, suggesting ways that you can learn to talk "childrenese."

GORDON, THOMAS,   *Parent Effectiveness Training*. New York: Peter Wyden, 1971.

This book highlights techniques of communication skills, particularly those kinds of statements designed to communicate understanding of feelings.

LOEFFLER, DOROTHY,   "Counseling and the Psychology of Communication," *Personnel and Guidance Journal* 48 (April 1970): 629–36.

Loeffler discusses the ways in which people communicate, the importance of communication in counseling, and describes six inappropriate or ineffective counselor-communication patterns. This is a "must" article for you to read and discuss.

Strong, Stanley, Ronald Taylor, Joseph Bratton, and Rodney Loper, "Nonverbal Behavior and Perceived Counselor Characteristics," *Journal of Counseling Psychology* 18 (November 1971): 554–61.

The authors studied counselors' nonverbal behavior and found that certain gestural, postural, and other nonverbal movements had a negative effect on how the counselors were perceived. The study suggests that there are inappropriate nonverbal behaviors of which the counselor must also be aware.

CHAPTER FIVE

Managing
the Counseling Session

We have discussed the qualities of a therapeutic relationship and how effective counselors attend to and understand the client. But we have not yet discussed the *structure* within which all this occurs. Experienced counselors enter each session with a sense of who they are, what they wish to do (or to be) in the session, and how they will represent themselves to the client. This is true of the first session and of the twentieth session. As we mentioned in the previous chapter, experienced counselors develop a personal style that they carry into the relationship. That style provides the structure, the directions for how to begin the process, how to develop it, and how to end or terminate it.

In this chapter we shall consider some awkward and sensitive times in the counseling relationship that require structure. Many counselors and clients have difficulty with beginnings and endings, whether they be the beginning or ending of a counseling interview or the beginning or ending of a counseling relationship. As you read the chapter, you will find suggestions and thoughts that may help you make smoother transitions into and out of these moments. There are two types of beginnings that will be examined: beginning the first interview you have with a client, and beginning subsequent interviews. Similarly, we examine the two types of termination: session termination and relationship termination.

THE FIRST INTERVIEW

Your first interview with a client will have a special set of dynamics operating. It is the beginning of a potentially significant relationship. As such, there are hopes and expectations, fears and reservations, acute awareness of some conditions and an amazing lack of awareness of other conditions—

all of which have a bearing upon the session. You might ask, "With so many emotional issues operating, how can I possibly have a successful first interview?" Counselors deal with this issue in one of two ways. Some counselors choose to work with the relationship dynamics that are operating. Other counselors choose to make the first session an intake interview and collect needed information about the client. Whichever choice you make, you must still attend to the other issue later. If you focus upon interpersonal dynamics in the first session, in the second or third interview you will want to collect information. If you use the first session as an intake session, soon afterward you must begin to acknowledge relationship dynamics.

If you wish to focus upon relationship dynamics, then the contents of Chapter 2 are particularly relevant. Specifically, you will want to achieve an accurate sense of the client's world and communicate that understanding back to your client. Learning to understand means putting aside your own agenda long enough to allow the client's world to enter your awareness. It means not worrying about yourself ("Am I doing the right thing?" "Am I looking nervous?" etc.). Until you have had the experience of several beginning sessions, this will be a difficult task. Of course, you will have an underlying set of objectives in this session:

1. To reduce your client's initial anxieties to a level that permits him or her to begin talking
2. To refrain from excessive talking, since that takes time away from your client
3. To listen carefully to what your client is saying and attempt to reconstruct in your thinking the world that he or she is describing
4. To be aware that your client's choice of topics give insight into his or her priorities for the moment

Initial Moments

In addition to these objectives, there are some logistics that require your attention. In opening the interview, be on time. This communicates respect. The beginning point can be as simple as a smile from you, along with a simple introduction and a motion to show the client where to sit. For example:

"Hello, I'm Bill Janutolo. Please have a seat here, or in that chair, if you wish."

After introductions, you might allow a brief pause to occur. This gives your client a chance to talk if he or she is prepared to begin. Or you might proceed to give the first interview some structure. There are questions that must be resolved. How long will the interview be? How do you want your client to address you? What should your client expect the sessions to be like? What are your client's rights? What will be your role? Answers to these and other questions provide the structure for the relationship.

Structuring has been defined as the way the counselor defines the nature, limits, roles, and goals within the counseling relationship.[1] It includes comments about time limits, number of sessions, confidentiality, possibilities and expectations, as well as observation and/or tape-recording procedures. Describing the counseling process and providing structure reduces the unknowns and thus reduces the anxiety of clients. It also permits clients the opportunity to check out their expectations.

You may want to emphasize the issue of confidentiality to new clients. Does it mean you will talk to no one? What are the implications if you are being observed by a supervisor or if you are tape-recording the session? Will you keep a written record? If so, what are the client's guarantees that the record will be kept confidential? Some of these may not be relevant issues, in which case it would be better not to introduce them as issues. You can discuss this with a colleague or supervisor to determine which issues are relevant and which are not. Here is how one counselor begins a session with structuring:

"We have about an hour together. I like to tape-record interviews with my clients. It's easier and less interfering than taking notes. I hope that won't bother you. I'm not sure what brings you here, but whatever it is that is bothering you will be treated in strict confidentiality. You can talk about anything you wish."

Encouraging the Client to Talk

After providing this initial structure, you and your client are ready to begin work. The obvious beginning is to get your client to talk, to indicate his or her reason for entering counseling, and perhaps to indicate in some form what he or she hopes to achieve as a result of counseling (the client's first statement of counseling goals). Your beginning will be an invitation to the client to talk. The nature of this invitation is important. A good invitation is one that encourages, but does not specify what the client should talk about. We call this an *unstructured invitation*. Some counselors refer to it as an *open-ended lead*.

Unstructured Invitations

The unstructured invitation has two purposes:

1. It gives the client an opportunity to talk.
2. It prevents the counselor from identifying the topic the client should discuss.

An unstructured invitation is a statement in which the counselor encourages clients to begin talking about whatever is of concern to them. For example:

[1] B. E. Shertzer and S. C. Stone, *Fundamentals of Counseling* (Boston: Houghton Mifflin, 1974), pp. 452–54.

"Please feel free to go ahead and begin."
"Where would you like to begin today?"
"You can talk about whatever you would like."
"Perhaps there is something particular you want to discuss."
"What brings you to counseling?"

By contrast, a structured invitation, one that specifies a topic, gives clients little room to reflect on the motives, goals, or needs that brought them to counseling. An example of a less desirable structured invitation to talk might be: "Tell me about what careers you are considering." The client is obviously tied down to a discussion of careers by this invitation, thus delaying or even negating a more relevant issue. (*Note*: If careers are what the client wants to discuss, an unstructured invitation allows this topic to emerge as well as a structured invitation would.)

The following exercise will help you develop the skills involved in initiating the interview.

EXERCISE: INITIATING AN INTERVIEW

This is a class exercise requiring a videotape system. Have class members select partners. Each pair is to decide who is to be the "interviewer" and who is to be interviewed. The exercise is to last for five minutes. The interviewer is to work toward achieving the following goals:

1. Set interviewee at ease (body relaxed, voice without tension).
2. Set self at ease (body less tense, open posture).
3. Get interviewee to start talking about anything (use unstructured invitation, silence).
4. Get interviewee to *identify* a current concern (acknowledge that the client came to counseling for a reason; ask about reason).

Following each exercise, reverse roles and repeat the procedure. Then, when all pairs have had the opportunity to do the exercise, replay the tape and discuss the encounters, using the following format:

1. Ask the interviewer's reaction to the tape.
2. Describe those behaviors that were good in the exercise.
3. Identify and describe those elements in which there is room for further growth.

FIRST-INTERVIEW OBJECTIVES

If your objective in the first interview is to focus upon client feelings or interpersonal dynamics, you will find yourself using responses that elicit feelings, describe relationships, and communicate your understanding.

These responses include restatement, reflection of feeling, summarization of feelings, requests for clarification, and acknowledgement of nonverbal behavior. These types of response encourage the client to present and explore thoughts and feelings, and give you an opportunity to understand some of the unique perceptions your clients may have.

On the other hand, you may wish to use the first interview to collect as much information as possible about your client, and not become involved with intrapersonal dynamics. This approach characterizes the intake interview and is based on the rationale that the more we know about the client's world, the better we are able to understand and respond to intrapersonal dynamics, particularly those perceptions that may be slightly distorted. An intake interview is highly structured. There are specific topics you want the client to discuss. The types of response that you will use in this interview tend to be probes, accents, closed questions, and requests for clarification, although the other mentioned responses may also be used on occasion.

COUNSELOR RESPONSES THAT ENCOURAGE CLIENT EXPRESSION

We have already described the unstructured invitation as a response to encourage the client to begin talking. It remains for us to describe the other responses that can be used in the initial interview, depending upon your purpose in that session. These responses are also used in subsequent counseling sessions and will be reintroduced in later chapters that describe specific objectives. First, let us consider those responses that are most useful when you focus on feeling and dynamics.

Restatement

Although it is important to maintain a listening role, there are certain kinds of response that communicate not only that you are listening, but also that you are a person with an active role. The *restatement* is one of these responses. It is a verbatim repetition of the main thought or feeling expressed by your client's preceding communication. An example is the following interaction:

> *Client:* "I don't know whether to stay in school or to drop out and get a job. But if I did drop out, I don't know what kind of job I could find."
> *Counselor:* "You don't know whether to stay in school or to drop out."

In this example, the client has communicated two thoughts: whether to stay in school and uncertainty about finding a job. When the counselor uses a restatement, it is easy to respond to the last thought emitted by the client, since it is the most immediate communication. However, this is a poor criterion. It is better to pick out the primary thought or feeling of the client's communication, regardless of its position in the statement. Just as a caution, it should be noted that the overuse of restatements produces a "parrotlike" effect in the interview. As a guide, the restatement can be used no more than about once or twice per topic without producing this mimic effect.

Reflection of Feeling

The *reflection of feeling* is a paraphrased response to a feeling communicated by the client, either verbally or nonverbally. The statement accomplishes precisely what its name implies: a mirroring of the feelings or emotion present in the client's message. Chapter 7 explores the different levels that this type of response can reflect. For our purposes in opening an interview, the following examples are sufficient.

Reflection of a verbally expressed feeling:

Client: "One of my main problems is that I need to come out of myself. And, uh, when I'm with people, or even when I'm alone, I have a loss for words. I have nothing to say; you know."

Counselor: "So when you are with other people, it must be a feeling like there's nothing inside you to come out and be noticed."

Reflection of a nonverbally expressed feeling:

Client: (Sitting in chair in slumped position, eyes downcast, forlorn look on face.)

Counselor: "From the way you look, you must be feeling pretty alone, pretty wiped out right now."

Summarization of Feelings

The summarization of feeling response is similar to the reflection of feeling, with one exception: It represents a set of feelings that might have been communicated over a period of minutes in the interview. Again, it is a paraphrase by the counselor that pulls together several feelings.

Client: "And that gets very uncomfortable, you know, with people. With a big group I'm fine, listening . . . or if I have something to say I get it out, usually. Usually, it takes me a very long time, and when I do come out, you see, I consider it's not worth saying and half the time, I think, I don't come out with it. Um . . . and that gets uncomfortable. And then I get the feeling like when I'm with people that if I can't be rambling off an awful lot of information, you know, then I'm not worth anything, you know? And that kind of thing bothers me."

Counselor: "Let me see if I understand all of that. In large groups you can feel a little safer sometimes if nobody notices you, but if you have something you want to say, it is so hard finding a way to say it that you finally decide it's probably not worth hearing if it's that hard to say. And that gets you to feeling down on yourself again."

Request for Clarification

Sometimes client responses sound cryptic or confused, and you are left wondering just what the client was trying to say. It can be very important to seek clarification in these moments rather than guessing or assuming that the communication was unimportant. The *request for clarification* asks the client to rephrase the communication. It can be stated in several ways:

> "Could you try to describe that feeling in another way? I'm not sure I am following what you mean."
> "When you say 'fuzzy,' what's that feeling like?"
> "I think I got lost in that. Could you go through the sequence of events again for me?"

Acknowledgement of Nonverbal Behavior

The nonverbal-behavior acknowledgement is a response that speaks to an obvious client gesture or posture without interpreting the meaning of the behavior. In this way, this response is different from the reflection of nonverbally expressed feeling. Although it is important that you resist any inclination to interpret the client's behavior verbally, you may speculate or ask for clarification of the nonverbal gesture. If the behavior has meaning, your client can tell you what the meaning is. Examples of acknowledgement of nonverbal behavior include the following:

> "You are holding your body really tight right now."
> "You look quizzical. Do you follow what I am saying?"
> "Your body is looking more relaxed now. Are you feeling more relaxed?"

COUNSELOR RESPONSES THAT SOLICIT INFORMATION

Since the intake interview is intended primarily to solicit information, the types of responses that characterize it include, but are not restricted to, those that follow.

The Probe

The probe is a question that requires more than a minimal or one-word response by the client. It is introduced with either *what, where, when,* or *how.* You will find that it is very difficult to ask questions that clearly place the focus upon your client. Fairly often, it happens that counselors ask questions that allow the client to respond with either a yes or a no. The result is that the client assumes no responsibility for the content of the interview. The purpose of the probe is to prevent this from happening. The following questions are examples of probes:

> "What are you thinking when you are silent?"
> "How do you plan to find employment?"
> "When do you feel anxious?"

The Accent

The accent is a one- or two-word restatement that focuses or brings attention to a preceding client response. It is said in a tone of voice that suggests that the counselor would like the client to elaborate. For example:

Client: "I'd like to have more self-confidence, but then I'd only be fooling myself."
Counselor: "Fooling yourself?"

Client: "After I returned from the meeting. I really felt dragged out."
Counselor: "Dragged out?"

The Closed Question

When your objective is to get the client to talk about anything, the closed question is not a good response. However, when you want the client to give a specific piece of information, it can be the best response available. For example:

"How old were you when your parents died?"
"How many brothers and sisters do you have?"
"What medication are you taking now?"
"Have you ever received counseling or therapy?"

The Request for Clarification

Requests for clarification can be used for soliciting information as well as for encouraging the client to elaborate about his or her feelings. It is important to keep in mind that such requests can be overused or underused. When overused, they can become distractors that repeatedly interrupt the client's train of thought. When they are underused, however, the counselor may have difficulty understanding what the client is saying. Sometimes the counselor is reluctant to seek clarification lest it impede or distract the client from the topic. If you are simply unable to follow the client's train of thought, it is more important to seek clarification than it is to allow the client to proceed. For example:

"Could you go over that again for me?"
"Could you explain that relationship to me again?"
"What did you mean a while ago when you said your parents were pretty indifferent?"

INTAKE-INTERVIEW CONTENT

While we have repeatedly described the intake as an information-gathering interview, we have not indicated what that information should be. This section presents a suggested outline of topics to cover and the rationale for their importance.

An assumption behind the intake interview is that the client is coming to counseling for more than one interview and intends to address problems or concerns that involve other people, other settings, and the future, as well as the present. Most counselors try to limit intake interviews to an hour. In order to do this, you must assume responsibility and control over the interview. No attempt is made to make it a therapeutic session for the client. The second session can begin to meet those needs. The following is a suggested outline to follow:

I.   Identifying Data
  A. Client's name, address, telephone number through which client can be reached. This information is important in the event the counselor needs to contact the client between sessions. The client's address also gives some hint about the conditions under which the client lives (large apartment complex, student dormitory, private home, etc.).
  B. Age, sex, marital status, occupation (or school class and year). Again, this is information that can be important. It lets you know when the client is still legally a minor, and provides a basis for understanding information that will come out in later sessions.

II. Presenting Problems, Both Primary and Secondary
It is best when these are presented in exactly the way the client reported them. If the problem has behavioral components, these should be recorded as well. The following questions can help reveal this type of information:
  A. How much does the problem interfere with the client's everyday functioning?
  B. How does the problem manifest itself? What are the thoughts, feelings, etc., that are associated with it? What observable behavior is associated with it?
  C. How often does the problem arise? How long has the problem existed?
  D. Can the client identify a pattern of events that surround the problem? When does it occur? With whom? What happens before and after its occurence?
  E. What caused the client to decide to enter counseling at this time?

III. Client's Current Life Setting
How does the client spend a typical day or week? What social and religious activities, recreational activities, etc., are present? What is the nature of the client's vocational and/or educational situation?

IV. Family History
  A. Father's and mother's ages, occupations, descriptions of their personalities, relationships of each to the other and each to the client and other siblings.
  B. Names, ages, and order of brothers and sisters; relationship between client and siblings.
  C. Is there any history of mental disturbance in the family?
  D. Descriptions of family stability, including number of jobs held, number of family moves, etc. This information provides insights in later sessions when issues related to client stability and/or relationships emerge.

V.   Personal History
  A. Medical history: any unusual or relevant illness or injury from prenatal period to present.
  B. Educational history: academic progress through grade school, high

school, and post–high school. This includes extracurricular interests and relationships with peers.

C. Military service record.

D. Vocational history: Where has the client worked, at what types of jobs, for what duration, and what were the relationships with fellow workers?

E. Sexual and marital history: Where did the client receive sexual information? What was the client's dating history? Any engagements and/or marriages? Other serious emotional involvements prior to the present? Reasons that previous relationships terminated? What was the courtship like with present spouse? What were the reasons (spouse's characteristics, personal thoughts) that led to marriage? What has been the relationship with spouse since marriage? Are there any children?

F. What experience has the client had with counseling, and what were the client's reactions?

G. What are the client's personal goals in life?

VI. Description of the Client during the Interview
Here you might want to indicate the client's physical appearance, including dress, posture, gestures, facial expressions, voice quality, tensions; how the client seemed to relate to you in the session; client's readiness of response, motivation, warmth, distance, passivity, etc. Did there appear to be any perceptual or sensory functions that intruded upon the interaction? (Document with your observations.) What was the general level of information, vocabulary, judgment, abstraction abilities displayed by the client? What was the stream of thought, regularity, and rate of talking? Were the client's remarks logical? Connected to one another?

VII. Summary and Recommendations
In this section you will want to acknowledge any connections that appear to exist between the client's statement of a problem and other information collected in this session. What type of counselor do you think would best fit this client? If you are to be this client's counselor, which of your characteristics might be particularly helpful? Which might be particularly unhelpful? How realistic are the client's goals for counseling? How long do you think counseling might continue?

In writing up the intake interview, there are a few cautions to be made. First, avoid psychological jargon. It is not as understandable as you might think! Avoid elaborate inferences. Remember, an inference is a guess, sometimes an educated guess. An inference can also be wrong. Try to prevent your own biases from entering the report.

USING INTAKE-INTERVIEW INFORMATION

Following the intake interview, but preceding the second session, you will want to review the write-up of the intake interview. Counselors develop different approaches to using this information. Some counselors look primarily for patterns of behavior. For example, one counselor noted that his client had a pattern of incompletions in life; for example, he received a general discharge from the army prior to completing his enlistment, dropped out of college twice, and had a long history of broken relationships.

This observation provided food for thought. What happens to this person as he becomes involved in a commitment? What has his client come to think of himself as a result of this history? How does he anticipate future commitments?

Another counselor uses the intake information to look for "signals" that suggest how she might enter the counseling relationship. Is there anything to indicate how the client might relate to females? Is there something in the client's life at present that common sense would suggest is a potential area for counseling attention; for example, is the client in the midst of a divorce; is the client at a critical developmental stage? The main caution is to avoid reading too much into the intake information. It is far too early for you to begin making interpretations about your client.

OPENING SUBSEQUENT INTERVIEWS

If your first interview was used to collect information about the client, it will be important to focus upon developing a therapeutic relationship in subsequent sessions. We refer you to the beginning of this chapter and to Chapter 2 for ways to develop this goal. Once you have established a relationship or rapport with your client, subsequent interviews will require that you reinstate the relationship that has developed. Reinstating the relationship usually amounts to acknowledging the client's absence since the last interview. This includes being sensitive to how your client's world may have changed since your last contact and your reactions in seeing the client again. This can be done with a few short statements, such as "Hello, _____. It's nice to see you again." This might be followed by some observation about the client's appearance: "You look a little hassled today," or "You're looking more chipper today." Or you might begin by asking, "How are you feeling today?" These types of questions focus upon the client's current or immediate condition and reduce the likelihood that the client will spend the major part of the session recounting how the week has gone. If your client needs a bit of small talk to get started, it probably means that he or she needs time to make the transition into the role of help seeker or help taker. The important point is that you probably will not need to go to the same lengths in establishing rapport as was necessary when counseling was first initiated.

TERMINATING THE INTERVIEW

The beginning counselor is often unsure about *when* to terminate, and may feel ready to conclude either before or after the client is ready. A general rule of thumb is to limit the interview to a certain amount of time, such as forty-five or fifty minutes. Rarely does a counseling interview need to exceed an hour in length, as both client and counselor have a saturation point.

There is also a minimal amount of time required for counseling to take place. Interviews that continue for no more than ten or fifteen minutes make it very difficult for the counselor to know enough about the client's concern to react appropriately. Indeed, counselors sometimes require five to ten minutes just to reorient themselves and to change their frame of reference from their preceding attention-involving activity to the present activity of counseling.

Acceptance of time limits is especially important when the client has a series of interviews. Research has shown that clients, like everyone else, tend to postpone talking about their concerns as long as possible. Without time limits, the presumed one-hour interview may extend well beyond an hour as a result of this postponing tendency. It is the one instance in which the client can easily manipulate the counselor.

Benjamin has identified two factors basic to the closing process of the interview:[2]

1. Both the client and the counselor should be aware that the closing is taking place.
2. Termination is concerned with what has already taken place; therefore no new material should be introduced or discussed at this phase of the interview. This can be a touchy situation for the counselor when the client suddenly introduces a new topic at the end of the interview. Generally it is best to suggest discussing the new material at the next interview when more time is available: "That sounds like a good place to begin next week." The rare exception to this would be when the client presents an urgent, immediate problem that he is really unable to handle.

Other Termination Strategies

Often a brief and to-the-point statement by the counselor will suffice for closing the interview:

"It looks as if our time is up for today."
"Well, I think it's time to stop for today."

This type of statement may be preceded by a pause or by a concluding kind of remark made by the client.

Another effective way is to use *summarization*. Summarization provides continuity to the interview, is an active kind of counselor response, and often helps the client to hear what he or she has been saying. It is essentially a series of statements in which the counselor ties together the main points of the interview. It should be brief, to the point, and without interpretation. An example of a counselor's using summarization at the end of an interview is the following:

"Essentially, you have indicated that your main concern is with your family— and we have discussed how you might handle your strivings for independence without their interpreting this as rejection."

[2] Alfred Benjamin, *The Helping Interview*, 3d ed. (Boston: Houghton Mifflin, 1981), p. 29.

Another possible termination strategy is to ask the clients to summarize; to state how they understood what has been going on in the interview, as in the following example:

"As we're ending the session today, I'm wondering what you're taking with you; if you could summarize this, I think it would be helpful to both of us."

Mutual feedback involving both the client and counselor is another possible tool for termination of an interview. If plans and decisions have been made, it is often useful for both the counselor and client to clarify and verify the progress of the interview, as in the following example:

"I guess that's it for today; I'll also be thinking about the decision you're facing. As you understand it, what things do you want to do before our next session?"

EXERCISES: OPENING AND TERMINATING THE INTERVIEW

Use the following triadic exercise to review styles of opening and terminating the interview. With one of you as the speaker, another as the respondent, and the third as observer, complete the following tasks, using the Observer Rating Charts printed below.

A. Opening the Interview

Speaker: Talk about yourself; share a concern with the listener.
Listener: Respond to the speaker as if you were opening an interview. Try out the responses mentioned in the chapter: unstructured invitation, silence, minimal verbal activity, restatement.
Observer: Observe the kinds of responses made by the listener. Keep a frequency count of the types of responses made. Share your report with the listener.
Recycling: If as the listener you did not emit at least two of the four response classes in your interaction with the speaker, complete the interaction again.
Role reversal: Reverse the roles and follow the same process.

B. Terminating the Interview

Speaker: Continue to explore the same topic you introduced in the above interaction.
Listener: Respond to the speaker as if you were terminating an interview. Try out at least one of the procedures mentioned in the section as approaches for termination of the interview (acknowledgement of time limits, summarization, or mutual feedback).
Observer: Observe the procedure for termination used by the listener. Share your report with the listener.

Recycling: If as the listener you did not emit any of the termination procedures, or if, for some reason, termination did not occur with your speaker, complete the interaction again.
Role reversal: Reverse the roles and follow the same process.

Record the order and frequency of responses used. If the counselor's first response was an unstructured invitation, place a "1" in the space provided. If the second response was silence, place a "2" in that space. If the third counselor response was a restatement, place a "3" in the appropriate space, and so forth.

Observer Rating Chart: Opening the Interview

COUNSELOR RESPONSE	ORDER
Unstructured Invitation	
Silence	
Restatement	
Reflection of Feeling	
Summarization of Feeling	
Request for Clarification	
Acknowledgment of Nonverbal Behavior	

Observer Rating Chart: Terminating the Interview

COUNSELOR RESPONSE	ORDER
Time Limits	
Summarization of Feelings	
Mutual Feedback	
Silence	
Structuring next session (Time, date, etc.)	

TERMINATING THE COUNSELING RELATIONSHIP

The process of terminating a counseling relationship can evoke various and even conflicting reactions for the counselor. Some may think of it as a "loss experience" if the relationship has been highly meaningful.[3] Others

---

[3] Rodney K. Goodyear, "Termination as a Loss Experience for the Counselor," *The Personnel and Guidance Journal* 59 (1981): 347–350.

may consider termination to be an index of the counselor's success.[4] From the client's point of view, termination may be a symbol of success or it may be a "recapitulation of the multiple goodbyes in life."[5] Whatever the interpretation, it is apparent that termination possesses an emotional dimension that can be intense.

Perhaps the most useful way to conceptualize termination is to think of it as a transition rather than an event.[6] As the counseling relationship develops and as the client is able to address and resolve the issues that necessitated counseling, the prospect of termination becomes a therapeutic stage in the process. More often than not, the counselor becomes aware of the approaching termination first. Concerns related to the timing of termination, the preparation for termination, and the anticipation of therapeutic problems related to termination become dominant in the counselor's mind.

When Should Termination Occur?

Some counseling theories provide guidelines for the timing of termination. These include such possibilities as letting the client determine the timing or having the counselor establish the date of termination at the outset of counseling.[7] Such issues will be dependent upon your own theoretical orientation. However, there are some pragmatic factors that contribute to the question of timing. Cormier and Hackney have summarized these pragmatic considerations as follows:

1. When counseling has been predicated upon a behavioral or other form of contract, progress toward the goals or conditions of the contract presents a clear picture of when counseling should end.
2. When clients feel that their goals have been accomplished, they may initiate termination.
3. When the relationship appears not to be helpful, either to the counselor or client, termination is appropriate.
4. When contextual conditions change—for example, the client or counselor moves to a new location—termination must occur.[8]

Preparing Clients for Termination

Clients should be made aware throughout the process of counseling that there will come a time when counseling is no longer appropriate.

---

[4] Robert H. Pate, "Termination: End or Beginning?" in *Counseling Adults: A Developmental Approach*, eds. W. H. Van Hoose and M. R. Worth (Monterey, Cal.: Brooks/Cole, 1982), p. 188.

[5] James C. Hansen, Richard R. Stevic, and Richard W. Warner, Jr., *Counseling Theory and Process*, 3d ed. (Boston: Allyn and Bacon, 1982), p. 306.

[6] L. Sherilyn Cormier and Harold Hackney, *The Professional Counselor: A Process Guide to Helping* (Englewood Cliffs, N.J.: Prentice Hall, 1987), p. 239.

[7] Ibid., p. 240.

[8] Ibid., pp. 241–242.

This does not mean that they will have worked out all their issues, nor will it mean that they have acquired all the tools and awareness necessary for a happy life. It does mean that they have grown to the point at which they have more to gain from being independent of the counseling relationship than they would gain from continuing the relationship. We take this position because we believe that human beings are happier and more self-fulfilled when they are able to trust their own resources. Of course, healthy people rely upon others, but they do so out of self-perceived choice rather than self-perceived necessity.

Occasionally you will know in the first session with your client that the relationship will last a certain length of time. For example, if your client is seeking premarital counseling and the wedding is to take place in two months, the time constraints are apparent. People going to university counseling centers may know that vacations dictate the amount of time allowed for counseling. In such cases, it is appropriate to acknowledge throughout the relationship that these time constraints exist.

When the relationship is more open-ended and determined by the client's progress, the termination stage begins well before the final session. It is our belief that for any relationship that has existed more than three months, the topic should be raised three to four weeks prior to termination. This allows the client time to think about and discuss the ramifications of ending counseling with the counselor.

Introducing Termination

Termination need not be presented as a major event. In fact, it is probably better to play it down rather than to play it up. If your clients' reactions suggest that it is a major event for them, then you can respond to that. But we find that it is better to acknowledge it as a fact rather than as an experience. This can be done by saying something on the order of:

> "We've been dealing with a lot of issues and I believe you've made a lot of progress. One of our goals all along has been to reach the point where counseling is no longer needed. I think we're reaching that point, and probably in about three or four weeks, we'll be stopping."

You can anticipate that your clients will have any of several reactions to this. They may feel good about their progress, nervous about the prospect of being on their own, sad to see a significant relationship ending, to name but a few reactions.

Occasionally it is appropriate to terminate gradually. This can be done by spacing the time between interviews. If you have been seeing your client weekly, change the appointments to every other week or once a month. Or you may schedule a "six-month check-in" that gives your client the sense of an ongoing relationship, one that leaves the door open, should that be necessary. Even with these gradual transitions, you will still have as a major concern the transition of a significant relationship.

Finally, it occasionally happens that the ending of a counseling relationship has a character of finality. Perhaps you or your client is moving. Or you may be referring your client to another help provider. In such instances there may be a grieving process connected with termination. It is appropriate to view this grieving process as necessary and therapeutic in its own right. It is a symbolic or ceremonious conclusion, an acknowledgment that the relationship had importance and that reality dictates that it end. In such cases, it is better not to hang on to it; that would only make the transition more difficult. If you are making a referral to another counselor, you must give up your role as helper for both ethical and practical reasons.

SUMMARY

While it is true that the experienced counselor has developed a style for managing the counseling session, beginning counselors must experiment with a variety of behaviors before a style begins to emerge. The verbal interventions included in this chapter are one way to begin defining that style. It is not assumed that all strategies will be comfortable or appropriate to every counselor trainee. Along the way, the beginning counselor is often confronted by misconceptions about helping, about client behavior, about expectations.

In Chapter 2 we introduced the notion of counselor intentionality as a dimension of the helping relationship. If you will recall, the intentional counselor is one who can function in the interview with alternative behaviors, and can conceptualize from different vantage points. These skills are particularly important in the initial interview and in opening subsequent interviews. In some counseling settings, an intake interview will be required. While the intake procedure is well-defined in terms of the type of information to be obtained, the counselor's skills in establishing rapport, soliciting relevant information, and reassuring the client require more than an outline of topics.

The skills of interview termination and case termination call for a counselor who possesses a repertoire of counseling skills and strategies. If termination is viewed as a transition from one psychological condition to another, the counselor functions as the bridge between those two conditions. Developing termination skills that are both natural to your personal style and effective in helping clients to make necessary adjustments will require time and experience. For the moment, it will suffice for you to understand the dynamics of the process and begin to address the matter of skill-building.

DISCUSSION QUESTIONS

1. Our communication patterns are learned from others, frequently from our parents. The rapidity of speech, the use of pauses or junc-

tures, the animation of speech can be attributed more to the influence of significant others than to the commitment of a communicated message. Who do you believe has been most influential in the evolution of your communication patterns?

2. What do you believe are the essential elements of a counseling relationship? As counselor, what are your contributions to the relationship?

3. Discuss what it might be like to be a client seeking help for the first time from an unknown counselor.

4. Discuss the positive perceptions that a client might have after going through an intake interview.

5. What do you think are the most important elements, from a counselor's perspective, in terminating a significant relationship? From the client's perspective?

6. Why is it not ethical to begin or to continue helping a client who is also receiving counseling from another therapist?

RECOMMENDED READINGS

BENJAMIN, ALFRED,   *The Helping Interview*, 3d ed. Boston: Houghton Mifflin, 1981.

Benjamin makes some important statements to the beginning counselor about beginning and terminating the interview, and relates his remarks to the counselor's role. You will find Chapter 2, "Stages," very helpful.

BRAMMER, LAWRENCE M., and EVERETT L. SHOSTROM,   *Therapeutic Psychology: Fundamentals of Counseling and Psychotherapy*, 4th ed. Englewood Cliffs, N.J.: Prentice-Hall, 1982.

Chapter 7, "Relationship Strategies and Methods," offers an extensive examination of such topics as opening the interview, identifying feelings, acceptance techniques, structuring techniques, listening techniques, leading techniques, and reassurance.

CORMIER, L. SHERILYN and HAROLD HACKNEY,   *The Professional Counselor: A Process Guide to Helping* (Englewood Cliffs, N.J.: Prentice Hall, 1987).

Chapter 11, "Termination and Follow-up," examines the conditions that affect the decision to terminate, the process of termination, and factors in making a terminating referral. It also provides a case example of termination.

DELANEY, DANIEL, and SHELDON EISENBERG,   *The Counseling Process*, 2d ed. Chicago: Rand McNally, 1977.

See especially Chapter 5, "Dynamics of the First Counseling Session," and Chapter 11, "Termination and Follow-up." Using counselor behavior as a point of departure, the authors have provided an excellent description of the characteristics and conditions that influence the opening and the termination of the interview.

FAST, JULIUS, and BARBARA FAST,   *Talking between the Lines*. New York: Viking, 1979.

This is a very readable little book on metalanguage communication and the message within the message. A good book for counselors to read.

KNAPP, MARK L.,   *Nonverbal Communication in Human Interaction*, 2d ed. New York: Holt, Rinehart & Winston, 1978.

Chapter 10, "The Effects of Vocal Cues Which Accompany Spoken Words," follows the material in this chapter. In particular, the reader will find the section on "Hesitations, or Pauses, Silence and Speech" to be informative and applicable to the counseling setting.

CHAPTER SIX

Responding to Cognitive Content

The counselor responds to the client in many ways, both verbally and nonverbally. Since your responses will have an impact on clients and the topics they discuss, it is necessary to be aware of the effect your responses will have. One very important effect deals with the changing pattern of the client's verbal behavior. As the verbal interaction and communication begin, topics arise; some topics are developed, some are modified, and some are diverted into new topics. As an active participant in the counseling process, you must be sure that your responses will influence the *direction* of topic development in such ways as choosing from among the topics that are to be discussed and the length of time allotted to the topics.

The purpose of this chapter is to acquaint you with and give you practice in recognizing different kinds of cognitive content, and in developing appropriate counselor responses for use with cognitive content. Responding to client content suggests alternatives and conscious choices that you will have to make in the interview. Then, when one choice has been made, the effect of that choice will become the basis for further alternatives. The following example will illustrate the types of choices you, the counselor, will be making. Suppose your client says:

Client: "I've known what this operation would do to my plans for a long time."

Your choices for responding are several. You could (1) paraphrase the client's remarks; (2) accent the word "operation" or the words "your plans"; (3) ask the question, "What will it do?"; (4) say "mm-hmm"; or (5) present an ability-potential type of response such as, "You are able to anticipate the consequences of the operation."

Obviously, these five stimuli will produce different responses from the client. The client may proceed to talk about the operation, about plans, or about how he or she "anticipates" events. In any case, your response would shape or mold the topic development, and, as a result, influence the future matters the client discusses.

In this chapter we will be working with content choices of a cognitive nature, as opposed to affective or feeling-type choices. In other words, the emphasis now is on your recognition and demonstrated ability to identify and respond to client thoughts or ideas dealing with *events*, *people*, or *things*.

RECOGNIZING ALTERNATIVES

Each comment of the client presents alternatives to you in terms of content to which you may respond. How you respond to one alternative will shape the next remark of the client. The counselor's task is to identify accurately the kinds of content presented by the client and the alternatives to which you, as the counselor, can respond.

EXERCISE: IDENTIFYING ALTERNATIVE TOPICS

To give you practice in identifying topic alternatives, read carefully the following client statements. Then identify and list all the different topics in each client response.

1. "They have, but I don't know just exactly how it does work, but you can sign up to take weekend trips in connection with the Air Force. It would be like duty because you have to qualify for it and you can travel all over the U.S."

   _____

   _____

   _____

   _____

   _____

2. "And I thought it was great. And I realize that most people have a bad opinion of women in the service but, uh, they shouldn't really, because a woman is going to be what she is, no matter where she is."

   _____

   _____

   _____

   _____

Feedback

The correct answers to the exercises above are as follows:

1. a. I don't know just exactly how it does work.
   b. You can sign up to take weekend trips in connection with the Air Force.
   c. It would be like duty.
   d. You have to qualify for it.
   e. You can travel all over the U.S.
2. a. I thought it was great.
   b. I realize that most people have a bad opinion of women in the service.
   c. They shouldn't really.
   d. A woman is going to be what she is no matter where she is.

RESPONDING TO ALTERNATIVES

The process of selecting alternatives can best be illustrated by excerpts from actual interviews:

   Client: "I like this type of a set-up where you can talk directly to people and talk with them. Uh, I don't like big crowds where I don't know anybody and they don't know me."
   Counselor: "You'd rather not be in big crowds."

In this example, the client's response contained two basic communications: (a) I like to talk directly to people, and (b) I don't like big crowds in which individuals get lost. The counselor chose to respond to the second communication in the client's response. Had the counselor responded by saying, "You prefer situations that permit you to get to know people," the topic focus would have been on getting to know people and the necessary conditions for this. As it was, the response led to a topic focus on the ambiguity of not knowing people. This does not necessarily mean that one response was more appropriate than the other; it is used only to point out the available alternatives.

A study of counseling typescripts suggests that when the counselor has alternative communications to which he or she may respond, the tendency is to respond to the final component of the response. Perhaps this is because of the immediacy of the final part of the response; but if so, that is a poor criterion. It is more logical that the counselor respond to the part of the client's communication that has greatest bearing on the client's concern and is therefore most important.

The counselor may also be tempted to respond to that portion of the client's communication that he or she finds most interesting. In this case the interview tends to center on those topics that the counselor may identify with or be dealing with personally. Again, the counselor must ensure that the choice of alternative topics reflects a decision about the client's needs rather than the counselor's.

TYPES OF DISCRIMINATING STIMULI

There are several types of responses you can use as stimuli to focus upon and elicit specific content expressed in the client's communication. The stimuli presented here can be used specifically to respond to cognitive content of the client's communication; that is, ideas that deal with *events*, *people*, and *things*.

Although these are not the only possible ones, four stimulus discriminators will be identified here for this purpose: silence, minimal verbal activity, restatement, and probe. Emphasis will be directed toward the latter two.

The use of silence and minimal verbal stimuli has already been noted in previous chapters. Their use as discriminators will be presented here briefly.

Silence

Silence affects the course of topic development as a discriminative stimulus by indicating that the counselor does not want to select or direct the topic at the given time it is used (see Chapter 4). Although the use of silence gives the counselor much less control over the direction topic development takes, it serves to increase the power of other types of responses. Thus, after you have remained silent for several moments, your next verbal response will be more valued by the client and, as a result, will have more influence in shaping the direction of topic development.

Minimal Verbal Activity

Minimal verbal stimuli are those verbalizations and vocalizations that people use when they are listening to someone else. The most common are "mm-hmm," "mmm," "yes," "oh," and "I see." They are unobtrusive utterances, but have a significant reinforcing value. That is to say, when an utterance such as "mm-hmm" is used consistently following a particular topic or word, the future occurrence of that particular topic or word increases.

Restatements

The restatement is the repetition of all or a selected portion of the client's previous communication, and neither adds to nor detracts from the basic communication. It confirms for the client that the counselor has heard the communication. Operationally, the restatement may be defined as a simple, compound, complex, or fragmentary sentence that mirrors the client's previous communication. It is dependent in its grammatical structure upon the grammatical structure of the client's previous response. The restatement can be used effectively so long as it is interspersed with other types of counselor responses. Otherwise, it can produce a "parrotlike" effect that has an adverse effect upon clients.

Some examples of restatements will help you understand this particular discriminative stimulus.

Client:	"I'm hoping to get a good job this summer."
Counselor:	"You're hoping to get a good job." (*Restatement*)
Client:	"It doesn't look like we'll get a vacation this summer."
Counselor:	"No vacation this summer." (*Restatement*)
Client:	"I like people but I sure get tired of them."
Counselor:	"You like people but you also get tired of them." (*Restatement*)

Now, try your hand with a few restatements:

    Client: "This has been a really rough year for me."

    You: _____

    Client: "Probably the worst class I have is literature."

    You: _____

Discuss your responses with someone.

Probes

The probe is a question that requires more than a minimal one-word answer by the client. It is introduced with *what, where, when,* or *how.* You will find that it is very difficult to ask questions that clearly place the focus upon your client. Typically, when you, the counselor, start asking questions, the client will give a mimimal answer and then wait for the next question. In other words, the client has not assumed responsibility for the content of the interview. The purpose of the probe is to prevent the client from answering questions with a yes or no response.

Some examples of probes include the following:

"What do you like about it?"
"What is keeping you from doing it?"
"How do you feel about it?"
"How is it helping you?"
"When do you feel that way?"
"Where does that occur for you?"

A probe can easily be overused in an interview. A beginning counselor often tends to bombard initial clients with questions. Extensive use of the probe in subsequent interviews can, however, give a "ping-pong" effect; the counselor asks, the client answers, and so on.

Try a few probes out for yourself.

Client: "It's hard to admit, but I really have wondered whether college is for me."

You: "_____."

Client: "I've gotten to the point where I can't do anything I'm supposed to do."

You: "_____."

Discuss your responses with someone.

EXERCISES: IDENTIFYING AND RESPONDING TO COGNITIVE CONTENT

A. Identifying Cognitive Content

To give further practice in identifying cognitive content—thoughts or ideas pertaining to events, people, or things—read carefully the following client statements. Then identify and list the different cognitive topics within each client response.

1. "I'm thinking about either going to grad school or getting a job—whichever would be better experience is what I'll do."

   _____

   _____

   _____

2. "People can say whatever they want about it, but as far as I'm concerned, my place as a woman is in the home and it will not change."

   _____

   _____

   _____

Feedback

The correct answers to the exercises above are as follows:

1. a. I'm thinking about going to grad school.
   b. I'm also thinking about getting a job.
   c. I'll do whatever provides the best experience.

2. a. People can say whatever they want to about a woman's place.
   b. I think my place as a woman is in the home.
   c. My opinion about this will not change.

B. Responding to Cognitive Content

The following exercise will give you practice in using the restatement and the probe. Read each client statement and then respond with the type of response indicated in parentheses:

1. *Client*: "Yes, I think that the best way to learn a language is to actually live with the people and learn it that way. Um, the first year that I was going back to Germany, I didn't learn very much at all."

   You: (*Restatement*) " _____

   _____ ."

2. *Client*: "I'd like to know the language, but still I can't carry on a conversation because it isn't used that much in my classes."

   You: (*Probe*) " _____

   _____ ."

3. *Client*: "I wanted to go back to school mostly because of the fact that I thought that there would be someone to lead because I just don't know which direction to go sometimes for a few things."

   You: (*Restatement*) " _____

   _____ ."

4. *Client*: "Well, I know you're supposed to study every night, which I don't do, but I'm not the only one who hasn't studied this semester. A lot of other kids have lost interest too."

   You: (*Probe*) " _____

   _____ ."

Discuss your responses with someone.

DISCRIMINATION AND SELECTIVE RESPONDING

The emphasis in this chapter has been on the selective responding to some client messages as opposed to others. When the client presents you with a multiple message, you can respond to all the messages or to only part of them. If you respond to only part of the client's messages, that part to which you don't respond will probably be dropped by the client in future communications.

EXERCISES: SELECTIVE REINFORCEMENT

A. Anticipating Client Responses

Using your responses to the client in Part B of the previous exercise, write what you think would be the client's following response to what you said. For example, with response 1, if you had said, "When were you in Germany?" the client might have responded, "I was there from 1969 through 1971."

1. Your response: _____

   _____

   Client's next response: _____

   _____

2. Your response: _____

   _____

   Client's next response: _____

   _____

3. Your response: _____

   _____

   Client's next response: _____

   _____

4. Discuss with another person how your stimulus caused the client to respond in one way rather than another. Did your stimulus discriminate between the various topics the client presented?

B. Observed Practice

With your triad, complete the following exercise:

1. One of you, designated as the speaker, should share a thought or idea with the respondent.
2. The respondent's task is to respond *only* to cognitive topics using only the four responses covered in the chapter: silence, minimal verbal activity, restatement, and probe.
3. The observer will use the Observer Rating Chart on p. 77 to keep track of the number and kinds of responses given. This feedback should then be given to the respondent.
4. After interacting in one triad for approximately ten minutes, reverse the roles.

Observer Rating Chart

COUNSELOR RESPONSE	TYPE OF COUNSELOR RESPONSE				
	Silence	Minimal Verbal	Restatement	Probe	Other
1.					
2.					
3.					
4.					
5.					
6.					
7.					
8.					
9.					
10.					
11.					
12.					
13.					
14.					
15.					
16.					
17.					
18.					

SUMMARY

In this chapter, we see that the counselor has numerous response choices, and each choice has a corresponding effect upon the client's following statement. In this reciprocal arrangement, both the counselor and the client influence the path that counseling will take in the session. Most therapists would acknowledge the importance of the client's choices, which reflect how the client conceptualizes problems and solutions, self and others, succeeding and failing, responsibility and control. However, they do not always acknowledge that the counselor similarly influences the session by choosing to respond to some messages rather than others, by exploring some issues rather than others, in short, by selecting what becomes the focus of the session.

These counselor choices are made in rather commonplace ways, including silence, minimal vocal utterances, restatements of the clients' message, and probing questions. The highly experienced counselor makes these choices almost intuitively; the inexperienced counselor must make these choices deliberately. If the inexperienced counselor relies upon intuition, the possibility of making bad choices is about equal to the possibility of making good choices. But what is more important, the inexperienced counselor who is unaware of, and thus is not deliberately making choices, is very likely to lack a sense of what is happening in the process of counseling.

This is the principal point of the chapter. Awareness of your effect through active choices allows you as counselor to maintain constant awareness of the process and, to some extent, the outcome of the session.

DISCUSSION QUESTIONS

1. What are some of the conditions that might work against you as you try to recognize the different messages in a client statement?
2. How can a counselor shape or influence the topical direction of a session without even being aware that he or she is doing so?
3. Under what counseling conditions might you want to have your clients talking about events, situations, or people, as opposed to feelings?

RECOMMENDED READINGS

FUQUA, DALE R., AL W. JOHNSON, MARK W. ANDERSON, and JODY L. NEWMAN, "Cognitive Methods in Counselor Training," *Counselor Education and Supervision* 24, no. 1 (1984): 85–95.

This article provides a good review of existing literature relevant to cognitive issues in counselor training.

SKLARE, GERALD, PEDRO PORTES, and HOWARD SPLETE, "Developing Questioning Effectiveness in Counseling," *Counselor Education and Supervision* 25, no. 1 (1985): 12–20.

The authors present a model for developing effective questioning skills. This article would be helpful to the counselor trainee who needs help either to understand the effect of questioning or to understand how some types of questioning are more effective than others.

CHAPTER SEVEN

Responding to Affective Content

What are some of the ways you communicate how you feel? When you're "down in the dumps," how does your voice sound? When you're angry, what is your face like? Your mouth? Your eyes? Your jaw? When you're afraid, what are some of the expressions you use to communicate this feeling? Human beings have many ways of communicating their internal states. The set jaw often is associated with determination. The glaring eyes speak for anger, even in the small child. The trembling voice, the soft voice, the downcast eyes—all have their meanings.

Clients use all of the verbal and nonverbal modes to tell the counselor of their problems. The emotions that accompany the narrative enrich and modify the message. They give the counselor the events of the client's world *and* the client's reactions to those events. These cues are not always easy to read. Clenched teeth can mean more than one thing. The trembling voice only suggests the presence of an intense emotion. A part of being a counselor is putting together the pieces or cues of the client's message in such a way that you can make reasonably good guesses about the underlying emotion.

As indicated earlier, the client's communication presents alternatives. In addition to alternative cognitive topics, you will find that you are faced with choices between cognitive topics and affective topics. This chapter focuses upon the affective message, how to recognize it, and how to reinforce its exploration by clients.

To review briefly, client communications that deal primarily with people, events, or objects may be described as *cognitive* details. Communications that reflect feelings or emotions may be described as *affective* details. Many messages contain both cognitive and affective components. When this occurs, the affective message may not be obvious in the words of the client. Instead, the feelings may be expressed through nonverbal modes, such as vocal pitch, rapidity of speech, bodily positions, and/or gestures.

VERBAL AND NONVERBAL CUES
ASSOCIATED WITH EMOTIONS

You may have wondered how you can identify another person's feelings. Although you cannot feel the client's feelings, you can infer what those feelings are and experience very similar feelings. That is to say, you may be able to know what it is like to feel a certain way. How do you do this? You draw from your own emotional experiences and recall that you, too, have experienced pain, anger, joy, and remember how they felt. You must first recognize the feeling in your client before you can reproduce a similar feeling in yourself.

To do this you may need to become more aware of, and sensitive to, certain verbal and nonverbal cues that are elements of the client's communication. Some of these cues are referred to as *leakage*[1] since they communicate messages the client did not deliberately intend to have communicated. Other cues, primarily verbal, are more deliberately intended and are more easily recognized and identified.

In the case of affective leakage, it is important to account for the inferences you draw. For example, when you say, "The client seems happy," that is an inference. If you say, instead, "The client is smiling, and that may mean that he is happy," then you have accounted for your inference.

The total impact of a client's message includes both verbal and nonverbal elements. The verbal impact means that there are certain nouns, adjectives, adverbs, and verbs that express the client's feelings about something or someone. For example:

"I am really *worried* about school."

The verbal element associated with the client's feelings in this example is the word *worried*. These kinds of words can be called *affect* words. They express some feeling that the client possesses. If an adverb such as *really* or *very* precedes the affect word, this indicates an even stronger intensity of emotion.

Nonverbal Cues to Affect

Nonverbal cues can be seen from such elements of the client's communication as head and facial movement, position of body, quick movements and gestures, and voice quality. Although no single nonverbal cue can be interpreted accurately alone, each does have meaning as part of a larger pattern, or *gestalt*. Thus there are relationships between nonverbal and verbal aspects of speech. In addition to the relationship between nonverbal and verbal parts of the message, nonverbal cues may also communicate specific information about the relationship of the people involved in the communicative process, in this case the counselor and the client. Nonverbal cues convey information about the *nature* and *intensity* of emotions, some-

---

[1] Paul Ekman and Wallace V. Friesen, "Nonverbal Leakage and Clues to Deception," *Psychiatry* 32 (1969): 88–105.

times more accurately than verbal cues. The *nature* of the emotion is communicated nonverbally primarily by *head* cues; the *intensity* of an emotion is communicated both by *head* cues and *body* cues.[2]

EXERCISE: IDENTIFYING BEHAVIOR

Pick a partner. Interact for about five minutes. Then each of you, in turn, describe your partner, using the phrase:

"I'm observing that you are_____."

Be sure to describe what you *see*, not how you think the other person feels.

TYPES OF AFFECTIVE MESSAGES

Although there are many different kinds of feelings, most feelings that we identify by words fit into one of four areas: affection, anger, fear, or sadness/depression.

Positive Affect

Feelings of affection reflect positive or good feelings about oneself and others and indicate positive feelings about interpersonal relationships. Many of them can be identified by certain affect words. Affect word cues that communicate the general feeling of well-being, affection, or satisfaction may be subclassified into five general areas:[3]

ENJOYMENT	COMPETENCE	LOVE	HAPPINESS	HOPE
beautiful	able	close	cheerful	luck
enjoy	can	friendly	content	optimism
good	fulfill	love	delighted	try
nice	great	like	excited	guess
pretty	wonderful	need	happy	wish
satisfy	smart	care	laugh(ed)	want
terrific	respect	want	thrill	
tremendous	worth	choose	dig	

[2] Paul Ekman and Wallace V. Friesen, "Head and Body Cues in the Judgment of Emotion: A Reformulation," *Perceptual and Motor Skills* 24 (1967): 711–24.

[3] Word lists for positive affect, fear, and anger are taken in part from T. J. Crowley, "The Conditionability of Positive and Negative Self-Reference Emotional Affect Statements in a Counseling-type Interview," (Ph.D. diss., University of Massachusetts/Amherst, 1970).

You can continue to add to this list of affect words related to affection. Can you begin to get the feeling for the message implicit in the usage of words such as these? Certain nonverbal cues often occur simultaneously with affection word cues. The most obvious of these cues are facial ones. The corners of the mouth may turn up to produce the hint of a smile. The eyes may widen slightly. "Worry" wrinkles disappear. Often there is an absence of body tension. The arms and hands may be moved in an open-palm gesture of acceptance, or the communicator may reach out and touch the object of the affection message lightly. When the client is describing feelings about an object or event, there may be increased animation of the face and hands.

Anger

Anger represents an obstruction to be relieved or removed in some way. Different kinds of stimuli often elicit anger. One such stimulus is *frustration*. Others are *threat* and *fear*. Conditions such as competition, jealously, and thwarted aspirations can become threats that elicit angry responses. Anger often represents negative feelings about oneself and/or others. Often fear is concealed by an outburst of anger. In such cases the anger becomes a defensive reaction because the person does not feel safe enough to express fear. Anger is also a cover-up for hurt. Beneath strong aggressive outbursts are often deep feelings of vulnerability and pain. Verbal cues that suggest *anger* may be classified into four general categories:

ATTACK	GRIMNESS	DEFENSIVENESS	QUARRELSOMENESS
argue	dislike	against	angry
attack	hate	protect	fight
compete	nasty	resent	quarrel
criticize	disgust	guard	argue
fight	surly	prepared	take issue
hit	serious		reject
hurt			disagree
offend			

You can continue to add to this list of affect words that suggest *anger*. Remember that anger covers a broad group of feelings and can be expressed in many ways. With the expression of anger, the body position may become rigid and tense, or it may be characterized by gross changes in body position or movement if the client is expressing direct dislike of the counselor or someone else in the room.[4] Sometimes anger toward another person or the self may be expressed by *hitting*, which consists of fault-finding or petty remarks directed at the object of the anger. For example, in counseling a couple with marital problems, one partner may

[4] Albert Mehrabian, "Communication without Words," *Psychology Today* 2 (1968): 53–55.

express this sort of anger by continual verbal attacks on the other person or by incessant remarks of dissatisfaction with the partner. Hitting can also be expressed through nonverbal cues such as finger drumming or foot tapping.

Certain vocal qualities are also associated with anger. Many times the voice will become much louder as the person becomes more rigid in what he or she is saying; if the anger is very intense, the person may even shout. In some instances of intense anger, the feeling may be accompanied by tears. Many times the expression of anger will cause vocal pitch to become higher. With some people, however, the vocal pitch actually is lowered, becoming more controlled and measured. This usually means that the person experiencing the anger is attempting to maintain a level of control over his or her feelings.

Fear

Fear represents a person's reaction to some kind of danger to be avoided. Often this reaction is a withdrawal from a painful or stressful situation, from one's self or from other people and relationships. As such, the person experiencing the emotions of fear may also be isolated and sad or depressed. Fear can also be described as a negative set of feelings about something or someone that results in a need to protect oneself. Verbal cues that suggest fear may be classified into five general categories:

FEAR	DOUBT	PAIN	AVOIDANCE
anxious	failure	awful	flee
bothers	flunk	hurts	run from
concerns	undecided	intense	escape
lonely	mediocre	unpleasant	cut out
nervous	moody	uncomfortable	forget
scare	puzzled	aches	
tense	stupid	torn	
upset	unsure		

You can continue to add to this list of affect words suggesting *fear*. Remember that fear is a broad category of feelings and can be expressed in many ways.

Several facial cues are associated with fear. The mouth may hang wide open as in shock or startledness; the eyes may also dilate. Fear may cause a furrow to appear between the eyebrows. Fear of the counselor or of the topic at hand may be reflected by the client's avoidance of direct eye contact.

Body positions and movements are also associated with the expression of fear. At first the person experiencing fear may appear to be still in body position or may draw back. However, after this initial period, body movement usually becomes greater as anxiety increases. Body movements may be jerky and trembling. Although parts of the body may shake, often the hands are tightly clasped as if giving protection. Tension may also be indicated through actions such as leg swinging, foot tapping, or playing with a ring or piece of jewelry.

Voice qualities are also indicators of the level of anxiety the client is experiencing. As the level of anxiety increases, the breathing rate becomes faster and breathing becomes more shallow. As anxiety and tension increase, the number of speech disturbances increases. This yields a greater number of cues, such as errors, repetitions, stutterings, and omissions of parts of words or sentences.[5] The rate of speech also increases as anxiety mounts, so an anxious person may speak at a faster than usual rate. The intonation of a depressed person or one in the grip of fear is also a departure from the normal intonation. The voice quality may become more subdued with less inflection, so that the voice takes on more of a monotonal quality.

Sadness

Some of the more common conditions expressed by clients are feelings of sadness, loneliness, or depression. These emotions may be a response to a variety of client conditions, including unsatisfying personal relationships, other environmental conditions, physiological imbalances or even diet. Verbal cues that suggest sadness, loneliness, or depression include the following:

SADNESS	LONELINESS	DEPRESSION
unhappy	alone	depressing
adrift	abandoned	depressed
sorrowful	isolated	disillusioned
distressed	missing	weary
grieve	missed	listless
heartsick		discouraged
		despondent
		gloomy

Sadness can also be expressed nonverbally. Cormier and Hackney have observed:

> Only the most preoccupied counselor will fail to notice some of the behavior correlates of sadness. Looking "down in the mouth," "whipped," or "about to cry," are common characteristics of sadness. Other physical cues include a poor posture or slouching in the chair, eyes averted downward and little

---

[5] G. F. Mahl, "The Lexical and Linguistic Levels in the Expression of Emotions," in *Expressions of the Emotions in Man*, ed. P. H. Knapp (New York: International University Press, 1963), p. 84.

eye contact with the counselor, talking in a monotone, staring into space, or a general lack of awareness or attention to personal qualities or to self-care.[6]

To summarize, the four main affect areas are those of *affection, anger, fear,* and *sadness/depression.* There are identifiable affect words and nonverbal facial cues, body position and movements, and vocal qualities associated with these feelings. Your awareness of these cues can assist you to identify with some accuracy the feeling state of your client and the affective components of his or her communications.

EXERCISES: IDENTIFYING AFFECT CUES

To give you practice in identifying nonverbal and verbal affect cues, complete the following exercises.

A. Identifying Nonverbal Affect Cues

Pick a partner. One of you will be the speaker; the other will be the respondent. The speaker should select a feeling from the following list:

Contentment or happiness
Puzzlement or confusion
Anger
Discouragement

Do not tell the respondent which feeling you have selected. Portray the feeling through nonverbal expressions only. The respondent must accurately identify the behaviors you use to communicate the feeling and should infer the feeling you are portraying. After he or she has done so, choose another and repeat the process. When you have portrayed each feeling, reverse roles and repeat the exercise.

B. Identifying Verbal Affect Cues

The speaker should select a feeling from the following list:

Surprise
Elation or thrill
Anxiety or tension
Sadness or depression
Seriousness or intensity
Irritation or anger

[6] L. Sherilyn Cormier and Harold Hackney, *The Professional Counselor: A Process Guide to Helping* (Englewood Cliffs, N.J.: Prentice-Hall, 1987), p. 118.

Do not inform the respondent which feeling you have selected. Verbally express the feeling in one or two sentences. Be certain to include the word itself. The respondent should accurately identify the feeling in two ways:

a. Restate the feeling using the same affect word as the speaker.
b. Restate the feeling using a different affect word but one that reflects the same feeling.

For example:

Speaker: "I feel *good* about being here."
Respondent: a. "You feel *good*?"
             b. "You're *glad* to be here."

Choose another feeling and complete the same process. When you have expressed each feeling, reverse roles and repeat the exercise.

C. Identifying Affective Components

Read the following client statements taken from actual interview typescripts and identify the affective component(s) in each statement by writing first-person sentences and by underlining the affect word of each client's communication. For example:

Client: "I'm not the type that would like to do research or, uh, things that don't have any contact directly with people. I *like* to be with people, you know— I feel at home and secure with people."

In this statement the affect word *like* is identified and the following affective components are identified by written sentences using the first person:

1. I enjoy being with people.
2. People help me to feel secure.

3. _____ .

If there is more than one affective component within a given client communication, place an asterisk (*) next to the one that you feel has the greatest bearing on the client's concern. In the above example, asterisk either 1 or 2, depending on which has the greater bearing in your opinion.
Client statements:

1. "Well, uh, I'm happy just being in with people and having them know me."
2. "And, and, uh, you know, they always say that you know some people don't like to be called by a number; well I don't either."
3. "In speech I'm, uh, well, in speech I'm not doing good because I'm afraid to talk in front of a bunch of people. . . ."
4. "I would love to go back to Germany; I think it's really fabulous."

VERBAL RESPONSES TO AFFECTIVE CONTENTS

It is too simplistic to say that the counselor communicates understanding of client feelings through attitudes such as empathy and positive regard. Although empathy and positive regard are necessary to the counseling relationship, the means for communicating these conditions also must be identified. Two primary reasons why the counselor may not respond to client feelings are (1) the counselor doesn't know what would be appropriate ways of responding, and/or (2) the counselor "blocks" upon recognizing the client's feelings.

Blocking refers to the counselor's reaction to client feelings in ways that reduce or restrict his or her helpfulness. For example, the counselor may accurately identify the client's feelings of anger but avoids responding to these feelings for several reasons. The counselor might be afraid that the client will leave if the interaction gets too intense. Or the counselor might not trust his or her own judgment and be afraid of turning the client off with an inaccurate response. Or the counselor might fear that acknowledging the feeling would produce a flood of more intense feelings in the client that would be difficult to handle. Or the counselor might have similar feelings that might be aroused. Client feelings related to sex, self-worth, and achievement are also potential blocks.

Knowing how to respond to client feelings with empathy and positive regard takes more than the possession of these attitudes. The counselor must make sure that these attitudes are communicated through words, statements, and timing. It is possible to identify certain counselor responses that will assist you to discriminate among affective contents, and communicate your understanding of the client's feelings at the same time. Two such responses are *reflection of feeling* and *summarization of feeling*.

Reflection of Feeling

The reflection-of-feeling response is distinctly different from the restatement response, but the two are often confused. As indicated earlier, the restatement is a paraphrase by the counselor of all or a portion of the *cognitive* content in a client's response, whereas the reflection is a paraphrase of the *affective* portion. The reflection of feeling accomplishes precisely what its name indicates: a mirroring of the feeling or emotion present in the client's message. When the client's response contains both cognitive and affective components, the counselor must differentiate between the two (see Chapter 8) in order to reflect the affective content.

The reflection-of-feeling response can occur at different levels. At the most obvious level, the counselor may reflect only the surface feeling of the client. At a deeper level, the counselor may reflect an implied feeling with greater intensity than that originally expressed by the client. The more obvious level occurs when the counselor reflects an affect message that is *overtly* present in the client's message by using a *different* affect word, but one that captures the same feeling and intensity expressed by the client, as in the following example:

Client: "I feel really mad that you interrupted me."
Counselor: "You're very angry about being interrupted."

The second kind of reflection occurs at a deeper level. This one mirrors an affect message that is only *covertly* expressed or implied in the client's message. Consider, for instance, the implied affect message in "I think we have a really neat relationship." The feeling inherent in the words refers to a positive affect message of *like, enjoy, pleased,* and so forth. Thus a reflection that picks up on the implied feeling in this communication might be among the following:

"Our relationship is important to you."
"Some good things are in it for you."
"You're *pleased* with the relationship."

This reflection that occurs at a deeper level not only mirrors the *covert* feeling but also must at least match the intensity of the client's feeling and perhaps even reflect greater intensity of feeling. Furthermore, the most effective reflection is one that emphasizes what it is the client *anticipates*; in other words, one that acknowledges the *implied admission* of the client's message. Consider this sort of reflection in the following example. Note that the counselor reflects back the covertly implied feeling with a greater intensity of affect and acknowledges the implied admission—that is, what the client would *like* to do or feel.

Client: "I feel like I have to be so responsible all the time. . . ."
Counselor: "Sometimes you'd feel relieved just to forget all that responsibility—to say 'to hell with it'—and really let go."

Although empathy and understanding of feelings are not themselves a panacea, they do serve some useful functions in the counseling process. For one thing, empathy enhances emotional proximity, creating an atmosphere of closeness and generating warmth. Secondly, empathy contributes to a sense of self-acceptance. When one person feels really understood by another, there is often a feeling of relief: "Gee, I'm not so confused and/or mixed up after all"; and a sense of acceptance about oneself: "This other person has understood me without condemning the way I think or feel."

When dealing with clients' emotions, beginning counselors often fall into certain traps. One trap deals with the counselor's own sense of security in handling the client's feelings. Many counselors, out of their own insecurity in the situation, will do inappropriate things that do not communicate their understanding of feelings. An example would be probing for further information. Here, rather than reflect the feelings, the counselor asks a question, as in the following example:

Client: "So, I'm wondering if you could help me find a new major—I suppose if I did find one I'd just bungle things again."
Counselor: "What was your old major?"

Although probes are often useful and information is often needed by the counselor, the *first task* should be to *communicate understanding of feelings*. An appropriate reflection-of-feeling response to the example above would be, "You feel that it's pretty futile to try again."

Two other common errors made in response to the client's feelings have been identified by Ginott:[7]

1. Responding to the event rather than the feelings involved
2. Responding to something general and abstract rather than specific

In the following exchange, the counselor errs by responding to the event:

Client: "I really felt left out at that party."
Counselor: "Did you go to the party with someone or by yourself?"

A better response would be to reflect the client's feeling:

"You might have felt alone there."

In the following exchange the counselor errs by responding to something general and abstract rather than specific:

Client: "I just can't seem to make it here at school with the courses."
Counselor: "They (the courses) can make you work."

It would have been better to respond to the client and not the courses, as in the following example of a reflection of feeling:

"You seem to feel pretty discouraged with school and all."

Summarization of Feelings

Summarization of feelings is very similar to reflection of feeling in that it is a response that discriminates between different affective components of the client's communication and communicates understanding of the client's feelings by the counselor. The basic difference in the two responses is one of *number*, or quantity. The reflection of feeling responds to only *one* portion of the client's communication, whereas the summarization of feelings is an integration of several affective components of the client's communication. Thus, summarization of feelings is really an extension of reflection of feeling. "However, in this case, the counselor is attending to a broader class of client response and must have the skill to bring together seemingly diverse elements into a meaningful Gestalt."[8]

Like the reflection of feeling, summarization of feelings involves reflecting the feelings of the client in your own words. Again, this involves

---

[7] Haim Ginott, *Between Parent and Child* (New York: Avon, 1965), pp. 30–32.

[8] A. E. Ivey et al., "Microcounseling and Attending Behavior: An Approach to Prepracticum Counselor Training," Part 2 *Journal of Counseling Psychology* 15 (1968): 1.

not just one feeling, but a bringing together of several feelings into a significant pattern. An example of summarization of feelings is the following:

Client: "The last few months I haven't felt like having any recreation at all. . . . I don't know why. . . . It just doesn't appeal to me. . . . Last night I almost had to force myself to go to a dorm party. . . . I used to go to all the dances when I first came to college, but now I don't care to."

Counselor: "You feel that even things that you were quite interested in at first now seem less and less interesting. . . . You don't know why that is, but it seems that way."

Summarization of feelings is often used instead of reflection of feeling when a client's communication contains many different affective elements, rather than just one or two. It can also be used effectively when the interview appears to be bogged down. For example, when one topic has been covered repeatedly, or when a dead silence occurs during an interview, summarization can increase the interview pace. By tying together various topics, summarization can identify a central theme. It also provides direction for the interview, and may thus furnish the needed initiative to get the interview going again.

EXERCISE: ANALYZING RESPONSES TO AFFECTIVE COMPONENTS

A. Responses to Client Statements

For the following counselor-client interactions, please observe the following directions:

1. Read each interaction carefully.
2. For each client statement, identify, by writing sentences, the various affective components of the communication.
3. For each client statement write your own response to the affective portion(s). Use both a reflection of feeling and a summarization of feeling for each client statement.
4. For each interaction, analyze the written counselor statement according to whether or not it is an appropriate response to the affective components of the client's communication. Then rate each of the written counselor responses on a scale from 1 to 5, with 1 being "completely inappropriate" and 5 being "completely appropriate."
5. Discuss the rationale for your ratings with someone else.

Client: "I don't mind school too much. I like it, you know, but I just want to get away and do something different."

Counselor: "School can be boring at times."

(1   2   3   4   5)

Reflection of feeling: _____

_____

Summarization of feelings: _____

_____

Client: "Actually I'm not looking for any kind of answer. It would scare me half to death if I got one. (Laughs) Then I would wonder what was wrong with me."
Counselor: "There's no need to worry about that."

(1 2 3 4 5)

Reflection of feeling: _____

_____

Summarization of feelings: _____

_____

B. Observed Practice

With your triad, complete the following exercise:

1. One of you, designated as the speaker, should share a personal concern with the respondent.
2. The respondent's task is to respond *only* to affective topics using only the two responses covered in the chapter: reflection of feeling and summarization of feeling.
3. The observer will use the Observer Rating Chart on p. 93 to keep track of the number and kinds of responses used by the listener. This feedback should then be given to the listener.
4. After interacting in one triad for approximately ten minutes, reverse the roles.

SUMMARY

The expression and development of affect is naturally assumed to be part of the process of counseling. However, this does not mean that the beginning counselor will be either comfortable with or sensitive to affective messages. Sometimes affect is implicitly expressed in the client's communication. Or there are times when one type of affect masks a different and perhaps more significant affect, such as anger masking fear. When these conditions exist, it is easy to miss the affective message.

In this chapter we have introduced verbal and nonverbal cues that suggest the presence of affect, the nature of affect, and how to respond

Observer Rating Chart

COUNSELOR RESPONSE	TYPE OF COUNSELOR RESPONSE	
	Reflection of Feeling	Summarization of Feeling
1.		
2.		
3.		
4.		
5.		
6.		
7.		
8.		
9.		
10.		
11.		
12.		
13.		
14.		
15.		
16.		
17.		
18.		
19.		
20.		

selectively to affect. The development of these counseling responses is closely related to the client's perception of counselor empathy. In other words, as you become more accomplished at recognizing affect accurately and responding to it, your behavior will be perceived as increasingly empathic. Reflecting and summarizing client feelings are two particularly helpful counseling responses in communicating your understanding to clients. This is not to suggest that you would want to respond to every perceived feeling. In Chapter 8, we shall consider the process of selective responding to affective or cognitive messages and the effect of your choices on the progress of the interview.

DISCUSSION QUESTIONS

1. When a client's message contains both cognitive and affective components, what conditions might lead you to respond to the affective element?

2. Although the reflection of feeling and the summarization of feeling were mentioned specifically as appropriate responses to affect, they are not the only appropriate responses. What other responses might be appropriate? Why would you consider them appropriate?

3. Often clients are less aware of their feelings than of their thoughts. How might you assist clients to become more aware of their feelings by the way you choose to respond?

RECOMMENDED READINGS

BRANNIGAN, CHRISTOPHER, and DAVID HUMPHRIES,   "I See What You Mean," *New Scientist*, May 1969, pp. 406–8.

The authors describe facial expressions and body gestures as "more primitive" communication than words, and categorize facial and body positions by the type of message being conveyed.

CORMIER, WILLIAM H., and L. SHERILYN CORMIER,   *Interviewing Strategies for Helpers*, 2d ed. Monterey, Calif.: Brooks/Cole, 1985.

Chapter 4, "Nonverbal Behavior," provides the most comprehensive review of client nonverbal behaviors that are encountered in the interview. Included in the chapter is an Inventory of Nonverbal Behavior (Table 4–1), which includes an exhaustive listing of kinesic, paralinguistic, proxemic, environmental, and temporal nonverbals.

EKMAN, PAUL, and WALLACE V. FRIESEN,   "Nonverbal Leakage and Clues to Deception," *Psychiatry* 32 (1969): 88–105.

The authors have drawn upon their extensive research to describe how our nonverbal behavior often gives away feelings that we think we are concealing.

————, "The Repertoire of Nonverbal Behavior: Categories, Origins, Usage and Coding," *Semiotica* 1 (1969): 49–98.

Ekman and Friesen present an excellent discussion of what they call *affect displays* and their relationship to behavioral consequences.

KNAPP, MARK L., *Nonverbal Communication in Human Interaction*, 2d ed. New York: Holt, Rinehart & Winston, 1978.

Knapp introduces Chapter 10, "The Effects of Vocal Cues Which Accompany Spoken Words," with a quotation from Shakespeare's *Othello* (Act IV): "I understand a fury in your words but not the words." He proceeds to discuss paralanguage and the meanings behind the meanings of messages. It is highly relevant reading.

MEHRABIAN, ALBERT, "Communication without Words," *Psychology Today*, September 1968, pp. 53–55.

Mehrabian distinguishes between verbal and vocal messages and also discusses facial expression and posture.

CHAPTER EIGHT

Differentiating Between Cognitive and Affective Messages

You have seen in Chapters 6 and 7 that there are many ways of responding to any client statement. Since your responses greatly influence the nature of topic development, you will be faced with the decision of which kind of content to respond to and, thus, emphasize. Very often, the client's particular response contains both a cognitive message and an affect message. Typically, in early interviews the affect message is disguised. The disguises may be thin but nonetheless necessary to the clients. It is their way of protecting themselves until they can determine what kinds of things you are willing to listen to. Once you are able to hear the affect message (and this comes with practice), you will have to make some decisions. It is important that you respond to that portion of the client's communication that you think is most significantly related to the client's concerns. The process of choosing between client cognitive and affective topics is called *differentiation*. Whether you choose to respond to the cognitive portion or the affect portion depends largely on what is happening in the interaction at that moment and on what the client needs. In other words, choosing to respond to the cognitive content serves one objective, whereas choosing to respond to the affect content serves another objective.

Some approaches (for instance, the phenomenological) favor almost an exclusive emphasis on affect, whereas others (such as rational-emotive, reality therapy) suggest that the primary emphasis should be on cognitive process. Of course, there are many variables influencing this sort of emphasis. In working with one client who intellectualizes frequently, the counselor may focus primarily on affect in an effort to get the client to recognize and accept his or her feelings. However, the same counselor, with another client who intellectualizes, may choose to emphasize cognitive elements if the counseling time is too limited for the client to feel comfortable with emotions after his or her primary defense has been removed. There are certainly times when emphasis on the affective takes precedence over the cognitive area and vice versa. Generally, though, during the interview process it is important to respond to both affective and cognitive topics. This is because, for all clients, there are times when feelings govern thought and times when thoughts and their consequences govern or influence feelings. The important point is not which comes first, but which type of counselor intervention is likely to be the most effective.

SETTING THE STAGE FOR AFFECT

In earlier chapters we noted that, at the outset, it is important to get clients to talk. Clients must be able to talk about themselves, identify and express feelings, identify their own behaviors, and relate to the immediate present. Strong feelings of vulnerability on the part of clients may prevent them from doing anything other than responding to their need for defending and protecting themselves. Reduction of these feelings can release energy previously used by clients for preserving their own image and make that energy available for growth and change. It is *only* at this point that clients can talk about themselves and identify and own their feelings and behaviors.

Thus, your initial objective, or first *process goal*, is to reduce the client's initial anxiety. Therefore, your first strategy with every client is an exploratory one; you must determine the effect your behavior has on the client by the client's initial responses to you.

Generally, responding to affect early in the counseling process is the best strategy for reducing client anxiety. This communicates your acceptance and understanding of these feelings to the client. However, with some clients who avoid emotion and intimacy, your response to their affect message may only induce greater anxiety. With this kind of client, you will have to modify the strategy and respond to cognitive topics; find out how the client thinks and what kind of ideas he or she has.

Counselors who always emphasize feelings to the exclusion of cognitive content impose certain limitations on the counseling process. Some of the limitations of responding only to feelings include the following:

1. Responding only to feelings is unrealistic and therefore reduces the possibility of the client's being able to generalize aspects of the counseling relationship to other relationships. For most clients it is highly unlikely that any of their friends or family would take only their feelings into account.

2. Responding only to feelings fosters an internal focus to the exclusion of the world around the client. Clients may become so preoccupied with themselves that the level of their other relationships deteriorates even more.

3. Responding to affect induces catharsis; that is, the ventilation of pent-up feelings and concerns. For some clients this may be all that is necessary. For other clients this is not a sufficient goal. With catharsis there is a greater possibility of reinforcing "sick talk"; that is, the counselor's responses to feelings may only generate more client negative self-referent statements.

On the other hand, responding primarily to cognitive content presents the following limitations:

1. It may reinforce the intellectualization process; that is, it may encourage the client to continue to abstract and deny feelings that are actually influencing his or her behavior.
2. It may not provide the opportunity that the client needs to share and express feelings in a nonjudgmental setting. The counseling relationship may be the only one in which a client can feel that his or her emotions (and consequently, the self) won't be misunderstood.

Again, it must be stressed that the initial strategy in the differentiation process is an *exploratory* one. All clients will respond differently to your emphasis on feelings or on cognitive content. Ways in which you may respond with discrimination to the client and some general effects of responding to affective and cognitive messages merit closer study.

TYPES OF DIFFERENTIATING RESPONSES
FOR COGNITIVE AND AFFECTIVE CONTENT

Several counselor responses are useful as discriminators for either cognitive or affective portions of the client's message. There are responses that can place emphasis upon one component of the message, to the exclusion of other parts of the client's response. Three particularly useful responses are the *accent*, the *ability-potential response*, and the *confrontation*.

The Accent

The accent is a one- or two-word restatement that emphasizes a very small portion of the client's communication. Its effect is that of a question or a request for clarification or elaboration. For example:

Client: "I'm having a hard time deciding which college to attend, uh . . .
              I'm not used to making decisions, so it's really perplexing to me."
Counselor: "Perplexing?" (Accents an affect word.)

What other words could the counselor have accented in this client response?

1. _____, which would emphasize: cognitive   affective

2. _____, which would emphasize: cognitive   affective

MODEL ANSWERS

1. "Hard time?"
2. "To you?"

Choosing "hard time" would have emphasized the affective portion, but accenting "to you" would have emphasized the cognitive part of the communication.

The use of the accent places emphasis on a particular thought or feeling. Usually it encourages clients to clarify or expand upon their previous statement, since it suggests that the counselor doesn't fully understand the client. It is used most appropriately to highlight a word that seems vague and abstract. Hence, it elicits specificity from the client.

The accent may be used to respond to either the affect or the cognitive message. The client must have used an emotionally laden word in his or her message in order for the counselor to accent the affect. This is one limitation of the accent. For example:

Client: "I don't think I will make the grades to stay here."

The counselor has no affect word to accent in this statement. However, the cognitive portion could be accented by saying, "Here?" (ACCENT). However, if the client said:

Client: "I'm afraid I won't make the grades to stay here."

Then the counselor could respond with "Afraid?" (ACCENT). The word *afraid*, which is an affect-type word, can be accented or emphasized, thus inviting the client to elaborate on his or her emotional reaction to the possibility of not doing well enough to stay in school. Try your skill with the accent in the following client statements:

1. *Client*:   "Things seem pretty bad now."

   You: "_____." (Emphasizing cognitive or affective?)

2. *Client*:   "I don't know what to do about it."

   You: "_____." (Emphasizing cognitive or affective?)

The Ability-Potential Response

The ability-potential response is one in which the counselor suggests to clients that they have the ability or potential to engage in a specified form of activity. It can be used either as a response to some cognitive portion or to some feeling expressed in the clients' communication. It not only reinforces the clients' sense of control and management of their own life and affairs, but also communicates the counselor's faith in the clients' ability to act independently. The ability potential can be used to suggest a course of action that is potentially beneficial to the clients as in the following exchange:

Client: "I don't know where I'm going to get the money to pay that bill."
You: "You could work for a semester and earn the money."

In other words, you are suggesting that the client has the ability or the potential to pay the bill, should he or she work for a semester and earn the money. Typically, the ability-potential response begins with "you could" or "you can." Like all of the other types of counselor responses that you have been learning, it can be overused. When that happens, it begins to sound unreal, hollow, and meaningless. It is used effectively as a means of identifying alternatives available to the client. It is misused when, in oversimplification, the counselor attempts to suggest or prescribe something as a panacea. The effect of this is to negate or hide the client's feelings of concern.

Make two ability potential responses in the following client statements:

Client: "I don't know what he'd do; I'm just hanging in thin air because I don't know how he feels about it."

You: _____

_____

Client: "I think I'd like to teach, but I don't know what the requirements and qualifications are."

You: _____

_____

The Confrontation

One of the most useful counselor responses is the *confrontation*. The word itself has acquired some excess emotional meanings. The confrontation is sometimes misconstrued to mean lecturing, judging, or acting in some punitive manner. A more accurate notion is to regard the confrontation as a response that enables clients to face what they want or feel they need to avoid. The avoidance might be a resistance to the client's own feelings or to another person, including the counselor and counseling relationship. The avoidance is usually expressed as one part of a discrepancy present in the client's behavior. Thus, the confrontation helps the client to identify a contradiction, a rationalization or excuse, or a misinterpretation.

The discrepancy or contradiction is usually one of the following types:

1. A discrepancy between what clients say and how they behave (the client who says he is a quiet type, but who talks freely in the interview).
2. A contradiction between how clients say they feel and how their behaviors suggest they are feeling (the client who says she is comfortable, but who continues to fidget).
3. A discrepancy between two verbal messages of the client (the client who says he wants to change his behavior, but who in the next breath places all blame for his behavior on his parents or on others).

Operationally, the confrontation is a compound sentence. The statement establishes a "you said/but look" condition. In other words, the first part of the compound sentence is the "you said" portion. It repeats a message of the client. The second part of the compound sentence presents the contradiction or discrepancy, the "but look" of the client message. For example:

"You say school isn't very satisfying, but your grades are excellent."
"You keep putting that job off, and eventually you're going to be back in the same trap of being mad at yourself."

The first part, or the "you said" portion, need not be stated by the counselor. It may be implied instead, if the client's discrepancy is obvious. For example:

Client: "I just can't talk to people I don't know."
Counselor: "[You say . . . (implied part)] But you don't know me."

Using the confrontation suggests doing just what the word implies and *no more*. The confrontation *describes* client messages, *observes* client behavior, and *presents* evidence. However, the confrontation should *not* contain an accusation, evaluation, or problem solution.

The confrontation serves several important purposes:

1. It assists in the client's achievement of *congruency*; that is, a state in which what the client says and how the client behaves correspond.
2. Its use establishes the counselor as a role model for direct and open communication. If the counselor is not afraid to confront these contradictions, perhaps the client can be less afraid of them.
3. It is an action-oriented stimulus. Unlike the reflection stimulus that mirrors the client's *feelings*, the confrontation mirrors the client's *behavior*. It is very useful in initiating action plans and behavior change on the client's part.

Try out the confrontation in these client statements:

Client: "I'd really like to take the course, but the grade contract is really tough."

You: _____

_____

Client: "I'm not really angry at my father; he's been doing this to me all my life."

You: _____

_____

Discuss your responses with someone.

EXERCISE: DIFFERENTIATING RESPONSES

A. Responding to Client Statements

In the client statements below, identify the *affective* and *cognitive* components of each; differentiate between the alternatives; then write an appropriate counselor response for each. Limit your responses to accent, ability potential, and confrontation. The type of response to use for each client statement is specified below in parentheses. Tell whether you responded to the affective or cognitive portion. Give your rationale for doing so.

Client 1: "On weekends I could stay here—I could probably get dates, but I don't stay here. I go home, or I go to my friends, 'cause I hate staying, just staying right here."
Counselor: (ACCENT)

Client 2: "I don't know how to act when I'm out on a date. I don't know what to do."
Counselor: (ABILITY POTENTIAL)

Client 3: "In speech, uh, I'm not doing good—the other day, uh, my instructor, he says to me, uh, you talk like you—like a whisper, as if you're trying to get away."
Counselor: (CONFRONTATION)

Client 4: "Most of the time, uh, well, I just like to be alone—but, uh, well, here it is really nice. I like being, uh, here. It helps me feel better."
Counselor: (ACCENT)

Client 5: "Well, I'm kind of interested in airport management—well, the book *Airport* really got to me, but I don't know very much about what that kind of job involves."
Counselor: (ABILITY POTENTIAL)

Client 6: "I mean I usually do feel much more comfortable alone—most of the time when I'm with someone else or, uh, with people, I just feel kind of clammy and nervous, you know."
Counselor: (CONFRONTATION)

B. Observed Practice

With your triad, complete the following exercise:

1. One of you, designated as the speaker, should talk about yourself with the respondent.
2. The respondent's task is to:
   a. Identify cognitive and affective topics present in the speaker's communication.
   b. Choose which topic you'll respond to.
   c. Respond using only the three responses covered in the chapter: accent, ability potential, and confrontation.
3. The observer will use the Observer Rating Chart on p. 103 to keep track of the number and kinds of responses used by the respondent. This feedback should be given to the respondent.
4. After approximately ten minutes of interaction, reverse the roles.

Observer Rating Chart

COUNSELOR RESPONSE	TYPE OF COUNSELOR RESPONSE		
	Accent	Ability Potential	Confrontation
1.			
2.			
3.			
4.			
5.			
6.			
7.			
8.			
9.			
10.			
11.			
12.			
13.			
14.			
15.			
16.			
17.			
18.			
19.			
20.			

EFFECTS OF RESPONDING
TO AFFECTIVE CONTENTS

The importance of responding to client feelings as an anxiety-reduction tool has already been mentioned. Generally speaking, responding to affect diminishes the intensity of feelings. For instance, responding to (accepting) strong feelings of anger expressed by the client will reduce their intensity and assist the client in gaining control of them.

The expression of feelings may be an important goal for some clients. Some people have had so little opportunity to express their feelings openly that to find an acceptant listener provides highly beneficial relief.

Responding to affect with acceptance and understanding can also assist clients to incorporate personal feelings and perceptions into their self-image. In other words, the counselor's acceptance of feelings that have been previously denied and labeled as "bad" by the clients suggests that they may have mislabeled these feelings, and thus, themselves.

Finally, responding to affect often is the best way to communicate your warmth and involvement with clients. That is, responding to client feelings establishes a high level of trust between you and your clients. It is precisely this kind of trust that enables clients to own their feelings, behaviors, and commitment to behavior change.

EFFECTS OF RESPONDING
TO COGNITIVE CONTENTS

We have already noted that responding to cognitive contents can be an anxiety-reduction tool for clients easily threatened by feelings. Thus, there are times when rapport with clients is established more quickly by discovering how they think before wondering how they feel.

Secondly, it is important to realize that behavior incorporates both feelings and thoughts. In order to effectively solve problems and make decisions, clients have to be able to think as well as to feel. Responding to cognitive contents assists clients in developing and expressing those thought processes involved in problem solving and decision making.

Because behavior is governed by thoughts as well as feelings, clients need to examine not only what they feel, but how they think. Behavior rigidity is often maintained by the kinds of thought patterns present in the client's repertoire. These may need to be discussed and explored before any behavior change can occur.

Although exploration of feelings is useful to most clients, it is often not sufficient for goal achievement. Once the counseling goals have been established, action plans must be developed to produce goal attainment. Responding to cognitive content goes one step further than responding to affect in that it focuses directly on behavior change.

Once your exploratory objective has been achieved and you have chosen when to emphasize affective content and when to emphasize cognitive content, it is time to develop and implement strategies for each of these areas. There are some strategies that are more effectively used in working with affective material. Other strategies are best implemented when the focus is upon behavior rather than feelings.

SUMMARY

In the first seven chapters the focus was upon skills that are basic to the helping relationship. In this chapter, we have introduced the process by which the counselor makes discriminations, sometimes subtle discriminations, that affect the outcome of a session. Choosing to respond to the cognitive dimension of a client's problems leads the session in one direction. Choosing, instead, to respond to the affective dimension leads in a quite different direction. Knowing which direction to take is close to the core of the therapeutic experience. In the remaining chapters we shall explore this therapeutic core in greater depth and detail.

DISCUSSION QUESTIONS

1. Every counselor has natural inclination toward feelings or thoughts. That is, when given an option, the counselor will respond to feelings (or choose to respond to thoughts) without thinking about goals. Which would be your natural inclination? What is it about your life, childhood, current wants, etc., that leads you to this inclination?
2. What do you think you will have to do in order to overcome your natural inclination? What are the conditions in counseling that would justify your responding to feelings, if your natural inclination was to respond to intellectualizations (or vice versa)?
3. If you were a client, would you prefer a counselor whose natural inclinations were toward feelings or toward rational thinking? What would be the advantages for you if you had the counselor you preferred? What would be the disadvantages to you with such a counselor?

RECOMMENDED READINGS

CUNNINGHAM, NANCY J., and NORMAN R. STEWART, "Effects of Discrimination Training on Counselor Trainee Response Choice," *Counselor Education and Supervision* 23, no. 1 (1983): 46–61.

This article reviews the training of counselor verbal responses and their relative value in the counseling process. The authors conclude that counselor training programs need to focus more directly on developing counselor skills relevant to later stages of the counseling process.

DOYLE, ROBERT E., "The Counselor's Role Communication Skills, or the Roles Counselors Play: A Conceptual Model," *Counselor Education and Supervision* 22, no. 2 (1982): 123–131.

Doyle defines the counselor verbal responses as subsumed under roles, such as *attender, clarifier, informer or describer, prober or inquirer, supporter, motivator, evaluator or analyzer*, and *problem solver*.

CHAPTER NINE

Conceptualizing Problems and Setting Goals

It is appropriate now to consider some of the larger issues of counseling, namely, the nature of client problems and the establishment of goals that are realistic antecedents to the solution of those problems. There are philosophical questions that underlie these issues, since there is no one way of conceptualizing human problems. We shall not be able to resolve the philosophical problems for you. It may require the greater part of your career to do that. But we shall present a viewpoint that represents our stand at this time. We find it useful because it focuses not only on our clients, but also on the world that they return to after each counseling session, a world in which the problems are real.

What brings clients to counseling? The answer to this, more than any other question, will reveal your role as counselor. It is a disarmingly simple question, but not one to be taken lightly. We begin with the response:

1. Clients enter counseling when they experience needs that they, alone, are unable to understand or to meet.

But that is only the beginning of an answer. Three processes have been identified and require further elaboration. These are *to recognize a need*, *to understand that need*, and *to meet that need*.

First, what does it mean to *need* something? It suggests that something is missing; that there is a hole, an emptiness. This condition reflects a dissatisfaction or incompleteness with the status quo. Something other than the status quo is required in order that the need diminish. Since any movement from the status quo involves *change*, implicit in the meeting of a need is a solution involving change.

This brings us to our second response to the original question:

2. The experience of *needing* is a natural part of the process of living and is the means by which we facilitate and enhance that process.

All human beings share certain basic needs. These include the need for security, nourishment, survival, affiliation, love, and self-esteem. Jourard has conceptualized these needs in a way that is useful for counseling.[1] They include the following:

1. *Survival needs*: Each of us is concerned with self-preservation and safety. This includes our psychological safety as well as physical safety. While we may not always recognize threats to our psychological safety, we do recognize our response to those threats, namely, increased anxiety, inaccurate or restricted perceptions of our world, and increasingly inappropriate behavior.

2. *Physical needs*: These include our need for nourishment, freedom from pain, rest, and replenishment of our energy. When these needs go unmet or become distorted (overeating, migraine headaches) our response may inhibit the satisfaction of still other needs (the migraine sufferer finds it difficult to achieve love and sex needs).

3. *Love and sex needs*: These are our needs to become involved in a close personal way with another human being. We grow in our development of these needs and often recognize their intensity only when we have suddenly experienced the loss of a close personal relationship. When these needs are unmet, we question our potential to love and be loved, to be in an extended relationship, or to be able to give to or take from another person.

4. *Status, success, and self-esteem needs*: These are the needs that motivate us to achieve in the eyes of our peers, to gain their respect, confidence, or admiration. When these needs are unmet, we lack self-respect, self-confidence, or we overreact with excessive and manufactured self-respect and self-confidence.

5. *Physical and mental-health needs*: When these needs are met, we feel like functional human beings. When they are unmet, we are incongruent, disillusioned, disoriented, and vulnerable to despair.

6. *Freedom needs*: These are our needs to feel autonomous, free to make our own choices, or free not to choose. When these needs go unmet, we feel restricted, undervalued, or unappreciated.

7. *Challenge needs*: These are the needs for activity, future orientation, opportunity. When they are missing, we are vulnerable to boredom, meaninglessness, or emptiness.

8. *Cognitive-clarity needs*: These needs reflect our drive to resolve the conflicts in values, ideas, and commitments that exist in our world.

Perhaps you would add to or take away from this list, according to your view of human beings. The point, however, is that all human beings experience needs as a part of living. To experience a need does not set a person apart as unusual, inadequate, or in some other way lacking. On the other hand, human beings are not always adept at recognizing (comprehending) experienced needs, nor do they necessarily possess the skills required to meet needs once the needs are recognized. To recognize and

[1] Sidney M. Jourard, *Personal Adjustment* (New York: Macmillan, 1963), pp. 33–38.

meet one's needs is not necessarily a natural part of the process of living; it must be learned.

This brings us to our third response to the original question:

3. The act of needing is a passive response that must be reframed into an active state, *wanting*, if the need is to be met.

The act of wanting requires not only that we acknowledge and comprehend the need we experience; it also requires that we conceptualize or fantasize something in the real world that would satisfy the need. It may be more money, a close friend, or a promotion. Until we are able to identify accurately a want, we are unable to mobilize our capabilities to remove the need. This process gives many people difficulty. Recognizing the difficulty, identifying the want that is related to the need, and developing a plan for obtaining the want is, often unknowingly, why clients enter counseling.

THE CLIENT'S WORLD

Thus far we have drawn a picture of the client as a person who is (1) continually experiencing needs, (2) not always understanding or even recognizing some of those needs, and (3) seeking your assistance when unrecognized and unmet needs become the bigger issue of living. Though this may be an adequate description of the person entering counseling, it fails to embrace the total situation of the client. Any description of clients must also include the world in which they live, including significant others, employment or the setting in which they spend the major portion of the day, expectations for self and others, habits and routines, dreams and fantasies of the future, attitudes toward the past, values and the meanings of life, and methods developed for survival (survival of responsibilities, tensions, disappointments, expectations of others, dashed hopes, etc.).

It is from the many dimensions of the client's world that needs arise. In the attempt to meet needs, often without understanding them as wants, the client arrives at solutions that are both inadequate and irrelevant. When this happens, an all-too-common situation arises: The solution becomes the problem. This can be illustrated by the person whose world is presenting so many pressures that sleeping becomes very difficult. After going to bed and lying there for an hour, the client decides to "try a new way to go to sleep." The solution may begin with counting sheep, thinking of "nothing," trying to relax muscles, getting another pillow, getting something to eat, changing the sheets, turning on the radio, turning off the radio, ad infinitum. With each new attempt, sleep becomes more elusive. What is worse, the next night becomes a set of expectations extracted from the previous night, and the solutions become more elaborate. Before long, we have more than a person with a lot of daytime pressures; we have an insomniac.

It is important for the counselor to understand, as well as is possible, the client's world. It is also important to understand the frustrated needs the client is experiencing in that world. It is vitally important to understand what the client has been doing or thinking to solve the problem of the unmet needs. We often find that clients have a very limited repertoire of solutions, and they apply these limited solutions indiscriminately. The result is a more complicated, less successful world than even before the "solution" was applied.

THE ROLE OF THE COUNSELOR

Based on what we have said about the client who is entering counseling, it follows that you would have some fairly clear responsibilities. These responsibilities are above and beyond creating a favorable climate for counseling, even beyond being a good and caring listener. It is your role to hear the unmet needs as clients describe their problems, and to help them hear those needs as well. It is then necessary to help clients translate these needs into wants in order that the working mode can be translated from a passive to an active one. You must listen for those solutions the client has tried that have become part of the problem, and help the client see this. Next, it is your role to help clients formulate goals that will help meet the needs. From these goals, plans of action may be constructed, implemented, and evaluated. Finally, you must help clients recognize that they are making progress. When clients have lived with problems too long, it is difficult to trust any progress.

If we might return to our insomniac client for a moment, we can illustrate the process. He appears to have multiple problems that include pressures as yet undefined as well as his response to those pressures—including his inability to go to sleep, which has become yet another problem. In addition to needing better ways of responding to and viewing the pressures, he needs a good night's sleep! The counselor can help the client recognize that the need for sleep is as real as the other needs, and is probably more important at the outset than the other needs. Translating this need into a want implies, accurately, that there is something the client can do to meet it. The counselor then must help the client see that his previous solutions to the insomnia problem have failed and should be discontinued. This is one of the many client problems in which an approach called *paradoxical intention* is likely to prove effective: Rather than have the client attempt to go to sleep, have him attempt to stay awake. It sounds preposterous to suggest that the way to achieve an objective is to attempt not to achieve it; yet it works, because in so doing, we do not introduce strategies that impede the solution.

After the insomnia problem has been addressed and strategies developed, there remain those pressures that led to the insomnia in the first place. Thus the counseling process may often be viewed as an unfolding process in which the outer, more obvious problems precede the more subtle, less obvious problems.

As we attempt to conceptualize or understand problem states, it is important that we keep in mind the client responses that can further complicate and add to the problem. These responses may be above and beyond the client's attempt to solve the problem. They include the following:

1. Attitudes the client may already have that contribute to the problem, impede the solution, or become the problem
2. Feelings, the emotional responses to the problem that often exaggerate the problem, impede the comprehension of the problem, or become the problem
3. Behavior, the habits and routines that are unthought or inappropriate responses, and perhaps contributors to the problem
4. Interaction patterns, those established ways of reacting to familiar others, including the miscommunication channels, expectations, self-fulfilling prophesies, etc.

Problem conceptualization does not come quickly. It comes progressively. After your first session with clients, you will begin to have some hunches about them, their world (and how they view it), and their problems (and how they view them). In subsequent sessions these initial hunches will be modified as you understand your clients better, and as your clients understand and report their world to you. There will be mistaken hunches along the way. These are to be accepted as part of the process, too. Acknowledge and discard them. The remainder of this chapter is an extension of the conceptualizing process; that is, conceptualizing the client's goals.

PROCESS AND OUTCOME GOALS

The counseling process involves two types of goals: *process goals* and *outcome goals*. Process goals are related to the establishment of therapeutic conditions necessary for client change. These are general goals, such as establishing rapport, providing a nonthreatening setting, and possessing and communicating accurate empathy and unconditional regard. They can be generalized to all client relationships and can be considered universal goals. Process goals are your primary responsibility; you cannot expect your clients to help you establish and communicate something like unconditional regard.

Unlike process goals, outcome goals will be different for each client. They are the goals directly related to your clients' changes, to be made as a result of counseling. As you are able to help your clients understand their concerns, you will want to help them understand how counseling can be used to respond to these concerns. The two of you will begin to formulate tentative outcome goals together. As counseling continues, the original goals may be modified through better understanding of the problems and through the development of new attitudes and behaviors that will eliminate or reduce problems. Goal setting should be viewed as a flexible process, always subject to modification and refinement. Most importantly, outcome goals are *shared* goals, goals that *both you and your clients* agree to work toward achieving.

Outcome goals that are visible or observable are more useful, since they allow you to know when they have been achieved. Yet not all outcome goals are stated as visible goals. For example, consider these two outcome goals:

1. To help your client develop more fully his or her self-actualizing potential
2. To increase the frequency of positive self-statements at home and at work by 50 percent over the next six weeks

Both of these could be considered to be outcome goals. They might even be so closely related as to be the same in terms of outcomes. Your clients may be much more attracted to such goals as developing their self-actualizing potential. You may want to view the development of self-actualizing potential as a composite of many smaller and more specific goals. To state it a little differently, self-actualizing is a hypothetical state that cannot be observed. It can only be inferred through certain visible and audible behaviors. Using this goal, you have no way of knowing the types of activity that your clients will enter into while proceeding toward the goals. As a result, you and your clients will know very little about what they could be doing in the relationship, and you will have no way of assessing progress toward the desired results. Consequently, the first goal listed above is not as satisfactory as the second, in that it does not provide you or your clients with guidelines for change.

When outcome goals are stated precisely, both you and your clients have a better understanding of what is to be accomplished. This better understanding permits you to work more directly with your client's problems or concerns, and reduces tangential efforts. Equally important are the benefits you are able to realize in working with specific behavioral goals. You are able to enlist the cooperation of your clients more directly, since they are more likely to understand what is to be done. In addition, you are in a better position to select viable techniques and strategies when your clients have specific objectives. Finally, both you and your clients are in a better position to recognize progress—a rewarding experience in its own right.

EXERCISE: GOAL SETTING

Tom is a junior in college. He is bright and personable, but a little shy. He came to counseling with the problem of relating to girls. Specifically, he believes that there is some flaw in his personality that "turns girls off." His reasons for thinking this grow out of his experience with dating. He reports that girls go out with him once or twice and then don't accept any more dates. He admits getting discouraged when he calls a girl for a date and she says she already has a commitment. If this happens twice, he never calls the girl again, assuming that she doesn't want to date him.

Identify a few goals which you think might be appropriate in working with Tom, given that you know very little about him.

_____

_____

_____

_____

_____

Are your goals specific or vague? How would you and Tom know when you had achieved these goals? Are your goals process or outcome goals? If they are process goals, would you need to involve Tom in their establishment? If they are outcome goals, how would achieving them affect Tom's dating problem?

What speculations could you make regarding Tom's solution to the problem? In what ways might his solutions add to the problem?

THREE ELEMENTS OF GOOD OUTCOME GOALS

Perhaps you have noticed from our previous examples that outcome goals are different from process goals in several respects. A well-stated outcome goal includes the following elements: the _behavior_ to be changed, the _conditions_ under which the change will occur, and the _level_ or amount of change. These elements apply to any outcome goal, whether it is to modify eating patterns, to reduce negative self-appraisal, or to increase assertive requests or refusals.

The second element of an outcome goal indicates the conditions under which the desired change will occur. It is important to weigh carefully the situations or settings in which the client will attempt a new behavior. You wouldn't want to set your client up to fail by identifying settings in which there was little hope for success. The client might agree to modify eating habits at home during the evening, but not to attempt to modify eating habits at the company dinner on Saturday night.

The third element of outcome goals involves the choice of a suitable and realistic level or amount of the new behavior. That is to say, _how much_ of the new behavior will the client attempt? Some clients enter diets with the expectation that they will reduce their consumption from 3,000 calories per day to 900 calories per day. A more realistic goal might be to reduce to 1,500 calories. This brings us to another thought about goals. As we modify goals, we come increasingly closer to the ultimate goals of the client. Each time we set a goal, it is a closer approximation of the results. Successive approximations are very important. They allow the client to set more attainable goals, experience success more often, and make what might be dramatic changes in life style.

EXERCISE: OUTCOME GOALS

In the following exercise, examples of client outcome goals are presented. Determine which of the three elements of an outcome goal—behavior, condition, or level—may be missing. After each example, list the missing parts, using *B* for behavior, *C* for condition, and *L* for level. Feedback will be provided to you at the end of the exercise.

The following example is provided as an illustration: to increase job placement (behavior) of physically handicapped clients seen in a rehabilitation agency (condition) by 30 percent in a one-year time period (level).

Identify the missing parts in the following six outcome goals:

1. To decrease temper tantrums
2. To increase exercise to two times a week over a six-week period
3. To decrease the number of nightly arguments at home with your wife
4. To decrease tardiness
5. To reduce aggressive behavior with sibling by 50 percent
6. To make three positive comments about the strengths of each member of your family during a one-week period

Feedback

1. The missing elements are the condition (*C*) and level (*L*) of the goal.
2. This goal specifies the behavior and the level; the condition (*C*) is missing.
3. The level (*L*) of the goal is missing.
4. This goal specifies the behavior; the condition (*C*) and level (*L*) are missing.
5. The behavior (*B*) is missing; "aggressive behavior" is a label and does not specify what the person would reduce.
6. This is a complete outcome goal! "Making positive comments" is the behavior; "three of them in one week" is the level; "to each family member" is the condition.

TRANSLATING VAGUE CONCERNS INTO SPECIFIC GOALS

Krumboltz and Thoresen have noted that rarely does a client begin by requesting assistance in achieving specific behavior changes.[2] Instead of saying, "I want to be able to talk to teachers without getting nervous," the client is likely to say, "I am shy." In other words, a personal characteristic has been described rather than the ways in which the characteristic is experienced. It then becomes the counselor's job to help the client describe the ways in which the characteristic could be changed.

Taking nonspecific concerns and translating them into specific goal statements is no easy task for the counselor. You must understand the nature of the client's problem and the conditions under which it occurs before the translation can begin. Even then there are difficulties. Krumboltz and Thoresen list seven stumbling blocks that counselors may face as they attempt to define behavioral goals:

[2] J. D. Krumboltz and C. E. Thoresen, *Behavioral Counseling, Cases and Techniques* (New York: Holt, Rinehart & Winston, 1969), pp. 7–8.

1. The client views his problem as someone else's behavior.
2. The client expresses the problem as a *feeling*.
3. The problem is the absence of a goal.
4. The problem is that a desirable behavior is undesirable.
5. The problem is that the client does not know his behavior is inappropriate.
6. The problem is a choice conflict.
7. The problem is a vested interest in not identifying any problem.[3]

What can you expect of yourself and your clients in terms of setting specific goals? First, the goals that are set can never be more specific than your understanding and the client's understanding of the problem. This means that at the outset of counseling, goals are likely to be nonspecific and nonbehavioral. *But nonspecific goals are better than no goals at all.*

Krumboltz describes these nonspecific, or general, goals as *intermediate* mental states, but he emphasizes that one cannot assume that such goals will free up clients to change their overt behavior.[4] The point is that, although intermediate goals may be necessary at the outset of counseling or until you have some specific knowledge of the client, such goals must be viewed as temporary. At the earliest possible time you must strive to identify more concrete and observable goals.

As you and your client explore the nature of a particular problem, the type of goal(s) appropriate to the problem should become increasingly clear. This clarification will permit both of you to move in the direction of identifying specific behaviors that, if changed, would alter the problem in a positive way. These specific behaviors can then be formulated into goal statements; as you discuss the client's problems in more detail, you can gradually add the circumstances in which to perform the behaviors and how much or how often the target behaviors might be altered.

After you and your client have established the desired outcome goal together, you can identify some action steps that might help the client to achieve the overall goal or target. These action steps can be thought of as *subgoals*. Subgoals consist of a series of smaller or intermediate steps or tasks that help the client perform the desired behaviors gradually. When several subgoals are identified, these are usually arranged in a sequence or hierarchy. The client completes one subgoal successfully before moving on to another one. By gradually completing the activities represented by subgoals in a successful manner, the client's motivation and energy to change may be reinforced and maintained. Successful completion of subgoals also may reduce potential failure experiences by giving the client greater control over the learning process.[5]

---

[3] Ibid, pp. 9–18.

[4] J. D. Krumboltz, "Behavioral Goals for Counseling," *Journal of Counseling Psychology* 13 (1966): 153.

[5] A. Bandura, *Principles of Behavior Modification* (New York: Holt, Rinehart & Winston, 1969), pp. 74–75.

EXERCISE: OUTLINING GOALS

Assume that a client, Nancy, has come to you for counseling. She describes her problem as a depressed state in which she can see no meaning in what she is doing, has no sense of where she is going in her life, and in general lacks a purpose in life. As you and Nancy probe the facets of her concerns, you can consider the specific changes Nancy would like to make. Gradually, these changes can be developed into an outline of desired goals. We refer to this as an outline because the major headings (I and II) represent the two overall or primary outcome goals for Nancy; the subheadings reflect the subgoals or activities Nancy might perform to achieve the overall goal gradually. Remember that goal setting is a flexible process, and that the goals listed in this outline might change as counseling with Nancy progresses.

   I. *Outcome Goal 1*: To identify the importance or significance of at least three daily activities in which Nancy participates at work and at least three daily leisure-time (nonwork) activities in which Nancy engages
      A. To monitor and log all daily work and leisure time activities for a week and to categorize these activities into pleasant and unpleasant tasks
      B. To increase Nancy's positive thoughts about at least three work-time and three leisure-time activities
      C. To decrease Nancy's negative thoughts about at least three work-time and three leisure-time activities
      D. To substitute and complete at least three rewarding activities for three unpleasant ones during the next week
  II. *Outcome Goal 2*: To help Nancy identify at least two long-range (5–15 years) purposes or directions and at least two short-term (present–5 years) purposes or directions to pursue in work and leisure time.

Complete the goal outline for this second outcome goal listed above. You might begin by establishing the criteria that Nancy would consider important. You might also consider having Nancy describe some of the people who appear to have this sense of direction. What do these people do that gives Nancy this impression or feeling? What could Nancy do to achieve her short- and long-range directions? From this kind of information and using your own imagination, construct the specific types of subgoals that would help Nancy implement this second outcome goal.

  II. *Outcome Goal 2*: _____

_____

_____

_____

_____

A. _____

_____ .

B. _____

_____ .

C. _____

_____ .

D. _____

_____ .

Notice the process by which outcome goals are established:

1. They begin as overall goals that are directly related to the client's specific or general concerns or descriptions of a set of problems.
2. Specific and observable subgoals are established which, if achieved, permit the realization of the overall goals.

Thus, goal setting moves from general to specific goals; the specific goals are directly related to the general goal, and the general goal is a reflection of the problems presented to the counselor.

CLIENT RESISTANCE TO GOAL SETTING

Occasionally a client may be hesitant about setting goals or reluctant to work toward change. For instance, upon completing a counseling session with her client, a counselor said, "This was the fourth interview, and I still cannot get him to talk about goals." When this happens, the counselor must deal with the question, "What is the client resisting?"

In working with client resistance to goals, it is helpful to realize that such behavior is purposeful. That is, what the client does or avoids doing achieves some desirable result for the client. Consequently, we may find that the client who resists setting goals may be protecting the behavior that is in need of modification because that behavior is doing something desirable. An example is the chronic smoker. While an individual may recognize the negative consequences of smoking, he or she also clings to the habit, believing that it is a helpful way to deal with a tense situation, that it is relaxing, that it increases enjoyment of a good meal, and so forth.

It becomes your task to get clients to identify what they gain from their current behavior. In so doing, you may determine whether that gain or outcome can be achieved in more desirable ways. For example, a young student may throw paper airplanes out the school window in order to receive attention from peers. Gaining attention may be a desirable outcome. It is the method that is the problem. Therefore, you and your client may consider more appropriate means for gaining increased attention, other than throwing airplanes out the school window.

Sometimes clients resist attempts to establish goals because they feel that the counselor (either overtly or subtly) is pushing them in a certain direction. Unless clients can determine some *personal* goals of counseling, the probability of any change is minimal. You can avoid creating client resistance to goals by encouraging active participation by clients in the goal-setting process.

CLIENT PARTICIPATION IN GOAL SETTING

Often, goal setting is construed to mean that you listen to the client, make a mental assessment of the problem, and prescribe a solution or goal. In fact, such a procedure is doomed to failure. The nature of counseling is such that the client must be involved in the establishment of goals. Otherwise, the client's participation is directionless at best and interferes with counseling at worst.

An example will illustrate this idea. A beginning counselor was seeing a client who was overweight, self-conscious about her appearance, reluctant to enter into social relationships with others because of this self-consciousness, and very lonely. Realizing that the problem of being overweight was an important factor, the counselor informed the client that one goal would be for her (the client) to lose one to three pounds per week, under a doctor's supervision. With this, the client became highly defensive and rejected the counselor's goal, saying, "You sound just like my mother."

Goal setting is highly personal. It requires a great deal of effort and commitment on the client's part. Therefore, the client must select goals that are important enough to make sacrifices to achieve. In the above example, the client's resistance could have been prevented if the counselor had moved more slowly, permitting the client to identify for herself the significance of her overweight and the importance of potential weight loss. At this point, both the counselor and client could then work together to determine the specific goals and subgoals that, when achieved, might alleviate the client's concerns. As with other aspects of the counseling relationship, goal setting should be an interactive process for which both you and your client assume responsibility.

SUMMARY

In this chapter, we have entered into the therapeutically active portion of the counseling process. In addition to the interactive process that takes place between counselor and client, the counselor begins to establish an internal analytical process in which the client's world is studied. That *study* is both within the client's context and in the larger context of healthy, productive living. Clients will become involved in this study, often quite naturally, as they unfold their experiences, feelings, and thoughts about themselves and others. Interwoven in this process is an emerging awareness of a different or perhaps better set of conditions, which become translated into *goals*. Some of these goals are related to the counseling relationship. Others are more related to the client's world. Through the recognition and establishment of these goals, the counselor begins to understand the direction counseling will take and can begin to help the client reach that same awareness. In Chapters 10 and 11 we will continue this exploration of the higher-order skills of counseling.

DISCUSSION QUESTIONS

1. In this chapter, reference is made to *process* goals and *outcome* goals. Identify and write down three process goals and three outcome goals for the insomniac client mentioned in the chapter. Share and discuss your goal statements with another class member.

2. Both the client and the counselor bring their worlds into the counseling session. We indicated that goal setting evolves out of an understanding of the client's world. How might the counselor's world affect that process of goal setting? Should the counselor be concerned about this issue? Why?

RECOMMENDED READINGS

BRAMMER, LAWRENCE M., and EVERETT L. SHOSTROM, *Therapeutic Psychology: Fundamentals of Counseling and Psychotherapy*, 4th ed. Englewood Cliffs, N.J.: Prentice-Hall, 1982.

For the reader who is unable to work within the context of behavioral outcomes, this book offers an alternative. Chapter 4 provides a useful description of how to facilitate client awareness, plan a course of action, and evaluate outcomes.

CORMIER, L. SHERILYN, and HAROLD L. HACKNEY, *The Professional Counselor: A Process Guide to Helping*. Englewood Cliffs, N.J.: Prentice-Hall, 1987.

The authors provide a discussion of the effect of goal setting on the client and offer a case illustration of goal setting in Chapter 5, "Developing Counseling Goals."

CORMIER, WILLIAM H., and L. SHERILYN CORMIER, *Interviewing Strategies for Helpers*, 2d ed. Monterey, Calif.: Brooks/Cole, 1985.

In Chapter 9, "Selecting and Defining Outcome Goals," the authors provide an in-depth examination of the process of developing outcome goals.

EGAN, GERARD, *The Skilled Helper: A Systematic Approach to Effective Helping*, 3d ed. Monterey, Calif.: Brooks/Cole, 1986.

Goal setting is one of the three dimensions of Egan's helping model. The reader will find a discussion of this stage, including how to construct a new scenario, critiquing the new scenario, and making choices and commitments on pp. 42–46.

CHAPTER TEN

Selecting Strategies and Interventions

The counseling process described in preceding chapters requires that you be able to make judgments during the interview about your behavior and its impact upon the client. This process of evaluation and decision making involves both a priori and post hoc activity. The a priori dimension requires that you understand both the client and the client's difficulties well enough to select a counseling intervention that has a *reasonable* chance of working. The post hoc dimension involves continuous evaluation of the client's response to your interventions.

Once specific client goals have been identified, your judgment and expertise are paramount. You must be able to establish rapport and a facilitative relationship. Beyond that, you must possess a repertoire of counseling strategies that can be used to help the client achieve the desired goals. These strategies become modi operandi, or plans of action that are designed to achieve specific counseling outcomes.

There are three major components of the strategy phase of counseling:

1. *Selection* of strategies
2. *Implementation* of strategies
3. *Evaluation* of strategies

The results of the evaluation of the strategies will lead either to termination of counseling or to selection of an alternative strategy. In some cases, the evaluation may indicate a breakdown in the relationship or the need for reassessment of the problem and the desired outcomes. This process of applying strategies is the subject of this chapter.

STRATEGY SELECTION

The range of counseling strategies is so broad that the beginning counselor can feel overwhelmed by the variety of choices that are available. Each counseling theory embodies its own set of techniques or interventions. For example, the Adlerian counselor relies heavily upon life-style analysis; the analytic therapist depends upon free association; the behavioral counselor uses successive approximation much of the time. But it would not be accurate to suggest that theoretical orientation restricts the types of interventions to use. Much of the recent professional literature points to the need to be eclectic in the choice of interventions, even while being consistent with a specific counseling theory. In other words, successful counselors are defined in part by their expertise with a wide variety of counseling interventions.

The process of strategy selection begins with certain assumptions. Cormier and Hackney describe these assumptions as related to problem definition and goal setting.[1] In other words, effective strategy selection cannot be made without first having a clear understanding of the problem and concrete counseling goals related to that problem. In addition to these considerations, other factors affecting strategy selection include the counselor's theoretical preferences, the counselor's level of experience and competence (some interventions should not be used by inexperienced counselors), and the counselor's knowledge of typical client responses to interventions.

In the selection process, several counseling strategies could be equally helpful or facilitating for a particular client goal. Hosford and deVisser make the point that "Just as there is no one perfect way to understand the client's problems, so there is no single perfect counseling strategy that fits all situations. Different techniques work differently for different individuals, for different problems, and for different goals."[2] If that statement makes the counseling process sound either too mystical or too complicated, then it should be noted that experience builds the counselor's repertoire of tools and insights. Few experienced counselors view the helping process as "mystical."

Finally, experienced counselors often discuss the use of strategies with clients. The purpose of this is to solicit client reaction and, perhaps even more important, to invite client cooperation in the intervention. Without soliciting client input, you might select a strategy that the client cannot or will not use. For example, some strategies require that the client engage in imagery or fantasy. Occasionally, a client is unable to participate in such an intervention, either because of an inability to generate vivid images or because certain phobic responses are triggered by emotive imagery. Yet another reason to discuss strategies with clients is to avoid potential

---

[1] L. Sherilyn Cormier and Harold Hackney, *The Professional Counselor: A Process Guide to Helping* (Englewood Cliffs, N.J.: Prentice Hall, 1987), p. 96.

[2] R. Hosford and L. deVisser, *Behavioral Approaches to Counseling: An Introduction* (Washington, D.C.: American Personnel and Guidance Association, 1974), p. 97.

values conflicts, either real or imagined. When the client perceives values conflicts, investment in the action plan may become minimal, or use of the strategy could create more problems than existed before.[3]

STRATEGY IMPLEMENTATION

Once you and your client decide on the strategies to use, you must consider ways to use the procedure most effectively. Effective implementation of a strategy may be influenced by three factors:

1. Sequencing of strategies
2. Rationale for a strategy
3. Instructions about a strategy

An initial decision must be made regarding the sequencing of the strategies. This decision is particularly important in cases where more than one procedure is used. As you may recall from Chapter 9, it is useful to establish priorities for goals and subgoals. In most cases, you will begin with strategies that are directed to the most important goal—the one that is most likely to relieve distress and also the one that the client is likely to attain successfully. If several strategies are used to meet this outcome, you and your client will decide which to use first—or whether to apply the strategies simultaneously. The main purpose for sequencing of goals and strategies is to help your client move toward the goal gradually.

Once the sequencing of strategies is decided upon, you will need to spend some time introducing a strategy. In all cases, the counselor should describe the strategy and the purpose of it to the client. Explaining the rationale may help the client to identify the value of a particular procedure. The degree to which clients consider their therapeutic strategies to be of value is a significant factor in determining the client's faith in counseling. You should also explore whether the client's expectations about change are realistic. You may need to point out that the strategy will not produce miracles, and that all change is achieved gradually.

Detailed instructions should also be provided about how the strategy will be used. Instructions should tell the client *what* to do, *how* to do it, and the *dos* and *don'ts* of strategy implementation. In some cases you may want to model the recommended procedure for the client. At any point in the process where the client gets bogged down or stuck, you can intervene to make any necessary adjustments.

Finally, you should help the client monitor the effects of the strategy in order to determine how well the procedure is working. If a strategy is not helpful, or if a client becomes turned off, a change may be necessary. A change in strategies usually will be dictated by some evaluation data about the procedure.

---

[3] Gerard Egan, *The Skilled Helper: A Systematic Approach to Effective Helping*, Monterey, Calif.: Brooks/Cole, 1986), pp. 264–65.

STRATEGY EVALUATION

One of the primary abuses of strategy application in counseling is the failure to monitor and evaluate the effects of the procedure. As Gottman and Lieblum note, "Too often, evaluation is done by consensus among professionals involved with the case when treatment terminates. . . ."[4] As a result, assessment is not substantiated with data, and the post hoc nature of the evaluation does not encourage flexibility in the strategy-implementation phase. Many counselors seem to regard data gathering as something unpleasant, and therefore something to be ignored. Yet, as Egan points out

> Tangible results form the backbone of the reinforcement process in counseling. If the client is to be encouraged to move forward, he must see results. Therefore, both counselor and client should be able to judge whether the action program is or is not being implemented, and to what degree, and the results of this implementation.[5]

There are generally three important factors to consider in strategy evaluation: *what* to evaluate, *who* evaluates, and *how* to evaluate.

Generally, you will want to assess together how much progress the client is making toward goal attainment. Unless specified otherwise, attainment of the counseling goals usually will be the standard criterion to use to measure progress or success. However, any side effects or lack of progress in using a strategy also should be noted. The relationship between the counseling goals and the evaluation process requires helpers to look for some rather specific behavior changes. In some instances, we would look for changes in overt behavior, such as reduction in cigarette smoking, improved communication with one's spouse, or more assertive skills. However, evaluation does not mean that private events or covert behaviors have to be ignored. Change in behavior may also mean change in thoughts or feelings.

Several sources of evaluation can be used to assess the effectiveness of a strategy. You and your client will be the primary sources of judgment about how well a strategy is working. You can determine how easily the strategy is being used by the amount of involvement it generates for the client, as indicated from the client's verbal and nonverbal behavior. However, the client must be the ultimate judge. A client's belief about a strategy can affect the results of the strategy. Moreover, particularly if the procedure is used outside the session, the client may be in the best position to determine how well the strategy seems to be working. Occasionally, counselor aides or significant others in the client's environment are also sources for evaluation.

Assessment may be done informally by oral reports and by observa-

---

[4] J. Gottman and S. Lieblum, *How to Do Psychotherapy and How to Evaluate It* (New York: Holt, Rinehardt & Winston, 1974), p. 2.

[5] Egan, *The Skilled Helper*, p. 225.

tions during the interview. Generally, we ask clients to give an oral description and analysis of the strategy by responding to these three questions:

"How comfortable did you feel with the strategy?"
"To what degree did you use the strategy during the week?"
"After trying it out, what is your opinion of it?"

In addition to this informal assessment, clients should be instructed to monitor in some way, either with a log or a tally, their progress toward the goals while the strategy is being implemented. Clients serve as their own control. This can be accomplished by a series of measurements of the goal behavior before, during, and after use of a counseling strategy. The measurements taken prior to the use of a strategy are referred to as a *baseline* or *base rate*. This indicates the *present* level of performance before any particular counseling intervention is introduced. As the strategy is applied, another series of measurements on the client's performance of the desired outcomes also is conducted. As Hosford and deVisser advise

Observations of the client's behavior near the termination point of counseling can easily be compared with the base rate data if the counselor records the same target behavior, in the same way, and for the same period of time as was done during the initial observations. This provides the counselor with an objective measure of the success of his learning interventions. If the data indicate that little or no behavioral change occurred, the learning strategies should be re-evaluated and perhaps changed.[6]

Without any more elaborate design, this simple series of measurements before and during the use of a counseling strategy can help the counselor and client evaluate the effects of the procedure. One limitation of this type of evaluation is that it does not rule out the possibility that something other than the counseling intervention contributed to or accounted for the client's change.

If the monitoring before and during a strategy reveals that clients are making progress toward the outcomes, these data become a source of motivation and encouragement. When all goals are achieved, counseling is normally terminated unless a new contract is worked out. If the monitoring indicates that little progress is being made, then a reassessment is necessary. You can use the evaluation data as feedback. Alternative strategies can be reassessed and may, with the client's consent, be implemented. If several strategies are used and all fail to produce much change, the data may suggest that there is another problem in the counseling process. Some necessary support or involvement may be missing in the relationship. Or perhaps the original problem assessment was incomplete. A valuable part of the defined problem may be missing. Perhaps another problem

[6] Hosford and deVisser, *Behavioral Approaches to Counseling*, p. 81.

area is really the concern. Still another possibility is that the client's original goals may need modification. Whenever goals are selected, there should always be flexibility to allow for subsequent revision of these objectives.

MULTIPLE STRATEGIES
FOR MULTIDIMENSIONAL PROBLEMS

Strategies are rarely used in isolation. Several different strategies or combinations of procedures may be necessary to deal with the complexity and range of concerns presented by a single client. As an example, suppose a counselor treats a client's alcoholism, but ignores the anxiety for which alcohol is used as a tranquilizer. The strategies used to decrease the drinking behavior may not be too effective unless the counselor and client also use strategies to deal with the client's limited coping skills, self-defeating thoughts, and environmental "payoffs" that maintain the drinking.[7]

As you may recall from Chapter 9, client problems tend to be multidimensional. Therefore, a client's goals may involve a variety of changes. Changes in covert behavior, such as thoughts, feelings, and attitudes, as well as changes in overt behavior and environmental events are all legitimate goals. Since thoughts, feelings, and overt behavior are interactive, a helper should keep in mind that both internal and external behavior change is important. Chapter 11 describes a variety of counseling strategies, some of which may be directed toward changing overt actions. Other strategies are used more often to modify thoughts, attitudes, and feelings.

EXERCISE: OBSERVED PRACTICE IN STRATEGY SELECTION, IMPLEMENTATION, AND EVALUATION

This role-play exercise is to be done by you and two other persons. One person should assume the counselor's role, another the client's role, and the third person can be the observer. Trade roles so that each of you can have an opportunity to practice the skills involved in selecting, implementing, and evaluating counseling strategies. Using the Observer Rating Questionnaire as a guideline, the observer can give you feedback about your performance. Answer the question by circling the correct answer. ("N.A." indicates that the question is not applicable.) It might be helpful to assume that you and the client already have established rapport and have defined the client's outcome goals. You can use this role-play practice to help the client consider and select some action strategies to meet these goals.

---

[7] F. J. Todd and R. J. Kelley, "Behavior Complexity, Behavior Analysis and Behavior Therapy" (Unpublished paper, University of Colorado Medical Center, 1972), p. 7.

Observer Rating Questionnaire

I. STRATEGY SELECTION

1. Did the counselor suggest some possible strategies to the client based upon the client's stated goals?

   Yes   No   N.A.

2. Did the counselor provide information about the elements, time, advantages, and disadvantages of each strategy?

   Yes   No   N.A.

3. Did the counselor involve the client in the choice of strategies to be used?

   Yes   No   N.A.

II. STRATEGY IMPLEMENTATION

4. Did the counselor suggest a possible sequence of strategies to be used when more than one strategy was selected?

   Yes   No   N.A.

5. Did the counselor provide a rationale about each strategy to the client?

   Yes   No   N.A.

6. Did the counselor provide detailed instructions about how to use the selected strategy?

   Yes   No   N.A.

7. Did the counselor verify if the client understood how the selected strategy would be implemented?

   Yes   No   N.A.

III. STRATEGY EVALUATION

8. Did the counselor explain why strategy evaluation is important and how it helps the client?

   Yes   No   N.A.

9. Did the counselor indicate the persons who will be involved in the strategy evaluation?

   Yes   No   N.A.

10. Did the counselor describe what the client should evaluate?

Yes   No   N.A.

11. Did the counselor explain how the client should obtain data about the strategy?

Yes   No   N.A.

12. Did the counselor verify whether the client understood the what, how, and why of the strategy evaluation?

Yes   No   N.A.

Observer Comments _____

_____

_____ .

SUMMARY

Chapter 9 focused upon the process of defining the direction counseling should take; this chapter addressed how to begin that journey and how to evaluate progress along the journey. There are many points of decision as strategies are selected, implemented, and evaluated. These decision points need not rest solely on the counselor's shoulders. Indeed, many skilled therapists believe that sharing this responsibility with the client not only enhances the process, but provides the client with additional growth experiences.

As you become more experienced in your practice of counseling, many of these steps will recede into the background of your awareness, allowing you to focus more on the immediate relationship variables that are present. For this to happen, you must develop good therapeutic habits, including questioning your participation in the process, questioning the progress that is being made, and involving the client in that process.

DISCUSSION QUESTIONS

1. From your frame of reference, what are the criteria you will use to propose counseling strategies to clients?
2. Discuss whether you believe there are some characteristics that distinguish between good and poor counseling strategies.
3. How would you introduce the strategy phase of counseling to a client?
4. Think of the benefits to be realized from evaluating counseling strategies. How would you describe these benefits to a client?

RECOMMENDED READINGS

CORMIER, L. SHERILYN, and HAROLD HACKNEY,   *The Professional Counselor: A Process Guide to Helping.* Englewood Cliffs, N.J.: Prentice-Hall, 1987.
In Chapter 6, "Selecting Counseling Strategies and Interventions," the authors discuss theoretical preferences, counselor experience, and typical client responses to interventions, and provide a case illustration of how strategy selection occurs within a therapeutic setting.

CORMIER, WILLIAM H., and L. SHERILYN CORMIER,   *Interviewing Strategies for Helpers: Fundamental Helping Skills and Cognitive Behavioral Interventions,* 2d ed. Monterey, Calif.: Brooks/Cole, 1985.
The authors present and describe guidelines for selecting counseling strategies in the overall helping process (Chapter 11) and common elements in strategy implementation (Chapter 12).

EGAN, GERARD,   *The Skilled Helper: A Systematic Approach to Effective Helping,* 3d ed. Monterey, Calif.: Brooks/Cole, 1986.
The third stage of Egan's three-stage model involves strategy selection. In Chapter 10, he discusses how the counselor can help clients develop appropriate strategies; in Chapter 11, he examines the choice process that involves formulation of action plans.

GOLDSTEIN, A., and N. STEIN,   *Prescriptive Psychotherapies.* New York: Pergamon, 1976.
In their introduction (pp. 3–24), the authors present some considerations to use in selection of therapeutic strategies.

HOSFORD, R., and L. DEVISSER,   *Behavioral Approaches to Counseling: An Introduction.* Washington, D.C.: American Personnel and Guidance Association, 1974.
Hosford and deVisser illustrate a way to compare the client's progress before and after counseling interventions in Unit 5 (pp. 79–94).

OKUN, BARBARA F.,   *Effective Helping: Interviewing and Counseling Techniques,* 3d ed. Monterey, Calif.: Brooks/Cole, 1987.
Chapter 7, "Applying Strategies," provides an excellent discussion of some criteria to consider when applying therapeutic strategies.

CHAPTER ELEVEN

Using
Counseling Interventions

In this chapter we shall examine a number of helping strategies or interventions. Those that are presented here have been selected both because they are used by counselors of varying theoretical orientations and because they enjoy some degree of empirical support. These strategies fall into four categories: social-modeling strategies, role-play and rehearsal strategies, cognitive-change strategies, and self-management strategies. They can be used to elicit feelings or attitudes, to help clients change feelings or attitudes, to identify inappropriate thoughts or behaviors, and to help clients develop more constructive thoughts and behaviors.

SOCIAL MODELING

Social modeling, based upon observational learning, refers to a process familiar to all human beings. If we are nothing else, we are observers. From earliest childhood, we humans watch and imitate. Through this vicarious experience, we acquire a great amount of knowledge and skills. The limitations to observational learning include the person's ability to observe, the attractiveness of the model, and the generalizability of the event to be learned.

As a helping strategy, *modeling* is used to help a client acquire desired responses or to extinguish fears—through observing the behavior of another person, the model. This observation can be presented in a live-modeling demonstration by the counselor, in symbolic form through written and media-taped models, or through the client's own imagination.

Live Modeling

Live models can include the counselor who demonstrates the desired behavior or teachers or peers of the client. Usually you will provide a modeled demonstration by a role-play activity in which you take the part of the client and show a way to respond or behave. Live modeling is particularly useful in instances in which the client does not have response alternatives available. The modeled demonstration provides cues that the client can use to acquire new responses. For instance, a client who wishes to acquire self-expression skills may benefit from seeing you or a peer demonstrate such skills in role-played situations.

Symbolic Modeling

Although live models have much impact on the client, they are often difficult to use because of the lack of control in ensuring their systematic demonstration of the desired behavior. To correct for this, many counselors make use of symbolic models through audiotapes, videotapes, or films in which a desired behavior is introduced and presented. For example, symbolic models could be used with clients who want to improve their study habits. Reading about effective study habits of successful people and their scholastic efforts is a first step to help clients specify those behaviors involved. Next, clients can listen to an audiotape or watch a videotape describing effective study behaviors.

Covert Modeling

Covert modeling is a process in which the client imagines a model performing a desired behavior or activity.[1] First, a script is worked out that depicts the situations and desired responses. For instance, if a client desires to learn to communicate openly with a spouse instead of avoiding issues, scenes would be developed that depict these situations and the responses the client wishes to make. For example:

It is a Friday night. You would like to go out but your husband (or wife) is very tired. You start to go upstairs and say nothing about your needs— but then you turn around and go up to _____ and say something like: "_____, I know you're pretty tired, but I sure would love to go out tonight, at least for a little while."

In addition to describing the situation and desired response, the scene also can include a favorable consequence.[2] The client could construct some probable positive outcome of the new behavior, or could think about some self-enhancing thought, such as congratulating oneself for the new behavior. Adding a positive outcome may reinforce the target response. However, the favorable outcome used should be something that is realistic and within the client's reach.

Following construction of these scenes, you can present each scene to the client by reading the script or by putting the script on an audiotape.

[1] J. R. Cautela, "The Present Status of Covert Modeling," *Journal of Behavior Therapy and Experimental Psychiatry* 6 (1976): 323–26.

[2] A. E. Kazdin, "Effects of Covert Modeling, Multiple Models, and Model Reinforcement on Assertive Behavior," *Behavior Therapy* 7 (1976): 211–22.

The client is asked to imagine someone who is similar. Typically, the client is instructed to imagine the scene several times, for about fifteen to thirty seconds. The client also is instructed to imagine the scene as intensely as possible. It is assumed that a person needs to have a fairly vivid imagination in order to use covert modeling effectively.

Characteristics of the Modeled Presentation

Regardless of the particular type of modeling procedure, you must carefully consider the way the model is presented to the client and the characteristics of the selected model.

The modeled presentation can affect the client's ability to attend to and remember the modeled demonstration. The first part of the modeled presentation should include instructions and cues about the features of the modeled behavior or activity. Prior instructions can minimize competition for the client's attention. A rationale for the use of modeling should also be given prior to the modeled display.

The scenarios or responses to be modeled should minimize the amount of stress in the presentation. Distressing and anxiety-provoking modeled stimuli may contribute to client resistance.

Complex patterns of behavior should be presented in modeled sequences. However, modeling of too many behaviors at one time may be overwhelming for a client. You can seek the client's input about the presentation of modeled responses to ensure that the ingredients and pace of the modeled demonstration are presented in a facilitative manner.

Practice of the goal behavior or activity increases the effectiveness of the modeling procedure. Practice may help the client code and reproduce the modeled behaviors. In addition to practice in the counseling session, you might assign homework to the client for practice outside the session. Self-directed practice can enhance the generalization of the modeling treatment from within the session to real-life situations. If a client experiences difficulty in performing a particular activity or behavior, instruction aids or props in the form of graduated hierarchies or counselor coaching can facilitate successful performance.

Characteristics of Models

In selecting models, it is best to maximize model–client similarity. Clients are more likely to learn from someone whom they perceive as similar to themselves. Such characteristics as age, sex, prestige, and ethnic background should be considered in selecting effective models. With some clients there is no better model than the client. Hosford and deVisser have found that arranging conditions so that clients see themselves performing the desired response can be a very powerful learning tool.[3] In their procedure, called *self as a model,* the client's desired behavior is demonstrated to the client on videotape or audiotape. For example, a client who

---

[3] R. Hosford and L. deVisser, *Behavioral Approaches to Counseling: An Introduction* (Washington, D.C.: American Personnel and Guidance Association, 1974).

wishes to stop stuttering listens to and practices with a tape in which all stuttering has been edited out. Hosford, Moss, and Morrell indicate that having a client observe both inappropriate and appropriate behaviors may weaken acquisition of the desired responses and promote occurrence of the undesired behavior.[4]

A coping model may be more helpful than a mastery model.[5] A client may be able to identify more with a model who shows some fear or some struggle in performing than someone who comes across perfectly. For example, a very shy, timid person could be overwhelmed by a very assertive model. This client may improve more quickly if exposed to a model who starts quietly and gradually increases assertive behaviors. Clients also may learn more from modeling when exposed to more than one model. Multiple models may have more impact on a client, because the client can draw on the strengths and styles of several different persons.[6]

When modeling fails to contribute to desired client changes, reassess the characteristics of the selected model(s) and the mode and format of the modeled presentation. In many cases, modeling can provide sufficient cues for the client to learn new responses or to extinguish fears. In other instances, modeling may have more effects when accompanied by practices of the target response. Such practices can occur through role-play and rehearsal strategies, as described in the next section.

EXERCISE: MODELING

Listed below are four hypothetical clients who might derive benefit from a modeling strategy. Based on the description given about each client, select the model that might be most effective for the client. Then check your responses against the feedback that follows.

1. The client is a black male in a graduate program who is avoiding a required statistics course because of his fear of math.
   _____ a. An older black male who has already made it successfully
   _____ b. A white male who has overcome his fear of statistics
   _____ c. A black male, about the same age, also enrolled in a graduate program that requires statistics

2. The client is a young, white, male veteran who lost a leg in combat and is trying to learn to get around in a wheelchair without soliciting assistance from other people.
   _____ a. A female who has been in a wheelchair since birth
   _____ b. A white male who also is a veteran
   _____ c. An older white male who is successfully employed

---

[4] R. Hosford, C. Moss, and G. Morrell, "The Self-As-A-Model Technique: Helping Prison Inmates Change," in *Counseling Methods*, ed. J. D. Krumboltz and C. E. Thoresen (New York: Holt, Rinehart & Winston, 1976), pp. 487–95.

[5] D. Meichenbaum, "Examination of Model Characteristics in Reducing Avoidance Behavior," *Journal of Personality and Social Psychology* 17 (1971): 298–307; A. E. Kazdin, "Covert Modeling and the Reduction of Avoidance Behavior," *Journal of Abnormal Psychology* 81 (1973): 89–95.

[6] Kazdin, "Effects of Covert Modeling," pp. 211–22.

3. The client is a middle-aged woman who is enrolled in a special treatment program because she is an alcoholic.
   _____ a. Another middle-aged woman who has successfully overcome alcoholism through this program
   _____ b. Another woman who is also an alcoholic
   _____ c. The woman's husband or a close relative

4. The client is a young woman who is institutionalized in a state hospital because she has refused to go out of her house, believing that people were after her.
   _____ a. Another institutionalized patient who is in the prerelease program
   _____ b. A staff psychiatrist
   _____ c. A female staff aide

Feedback

1. Probably the best choice would be *c*. This model would be similar to the client in race, age, sex, and educational goals.
2. We would choose model *b*, who, even though he is not in a wheelchair, is similar to the client in race, age, sex, and can identify with the cause of the client's disability since he is also a veteran.
3. Model *a*, who is similar to the client in age, race, sex, and problem.
4. Model *a*, who is similar to the client in terms of the patient status but has been able to deal with the problems to the point of being near release from the institution.

ROLE-PLAY AND REHEARSAL

Role-play and rehearsal strategies promote behavior change through simulated or in vivo enactment of desired responses. Common elements in the application of role-play and rehearsal strategies include the following:

1. A reenactment of oneself, another person, an event, or a set of responses by the client
2. The use of the present, or the "here and now," to carry out the reenactment
3. A gradual shaping process in which less difficult scenes are enacted first, and more difficult scenes are reserved for later
4. Feedback to the client by the counselor and/or other adjunct persons.

Depending on the therapeutic goal, role-playing procedures often are used by dynamic therapies as a method to achieve catharsis, by insight therapies as a means to bring about attitudinal changes, by Gestalt therapy as a tool to promote conflict resolution and self-awareness, and by behavior therapy as a way to facilitate behavior change.

Role Play as a Method of Attitude Change

As a method of attitude change, role play relies heavily on role reversal. The client may be asked to play the role of a certain person in a specified situation, or to play the role of someone with opposing beliefs. Recent research indicates that role reversal can help a person reevaluate the intentions of the other person and become more understanding of the other person's position.[7]

Following role reversal, clients may be more receptive to modifying their own attitudes. Apparently, the taking of another's role is the element that produces change; listening to someone else present an opposing belief seems only to strengthen each person's existing attitudes.[8] Also, the ability to really become involved in the role is a factor influencing the success of the role reversal.[9]

EXERCISE: ROLE REVERSAL

The following exercise may give you some exposure to using role play and role reversal to examine your attitudes and beliefs about a situation or an event.

With another person, identify a topic that each of you is willing to discuss and about which each of you holds opposing or conflicting beliefs. For example, one of you might favor abortion, and the other might oppose it. Or one of you might support legalization of marijuana, and the other does not. Or, one of you believes that one theory of counseling is the "only" theory, and the other person disagrees. *Briefly* state your position to each other. The purpose of this initial statement is only to inform the other person of your belief. Do not argue or stack the conversation in your favor; simply state your position on the matter. After you are aware of the other person's attitude about the issue, try out Johnson's instructions for role reversal:

> Switch roles with the other representative and present his/her position as if you were he/she. It is important in reversing roles that you are as *sincere and emotionally involved* in the other's role as possible. It is also important that you present as *complete and full a restatement* of the other's position as you can. . . . Feel free to *improvise* new ideas which support the other's position as you reverse roles and to *be creative* in the way in which you present his/her position. . . .[10]

Role Play as a Method of Self-Awareness and Conflict Resolution

As a method of self-awareness and conflict resolution, role play may help the client experience a situation rather than merely talk about it.

---

[7] A. C. Bohart, "Role Playing and Interpersonal Conflict Reduction," *Journal of Counseling Psychology* 24 (1977): 15–24.

[8] D. W. Johnson, "Effectivenesss of Role Reversal: Actor or Listener," *Psychological Reports* 28 (1971): 275–82.

[9] Ibid.

[10] Ibid., p. 279.

Bohart points out that role playing may elicit feelings in the client that are similar in nature and intensity to those experienced in an actual situation.[11] Role playing may provide an opportunity for insight and for expression of affect. In counseling, role playing might be introduced as a method to heighten clients' awareness of their feelings about situations. One of the major ways in which role playing can be used to resolve conflicts and to increase self-awareness is through a dialogue.

For example, clients may report conflicts in their feelings or thoughts, or in relationships with other significant people. Often, having a client identify various alternatives and their consequences may reveal that the client is stuck at the point of decision. For example, the client may say:

> "I just don't know what to do. I'd like to go with him, but then I also think I should stay here."

Or the client may express hesitation about taking some action because of the possible effects on another person:

> "I just can't change majors. I'm afraid it would really bother my folks."

A useful role-play tool in these kinds of situations is the *dialogue*, which involves having the client take the part of each person or each side of the argument. The client is asked to "play out" the conflict through an imaginary dialogue. In the first example above, the client is encouraged to talk to both parts of the self. The dialogue between the two selves, which occurs in present-tense form, is continued until one part of the conflict outweighs the other.

In the example involving a second person, the client is instructed to "put the other person in the chair across from you and imagine he or she is there." The client begins the dialogue by expressing wants and resentments about the other person. Then the client changes chairs, becomes the other person, and responds to what was just said. The client assumes the first role again and responds to the other person. Having a dialogue in this manner not ony serves as practice for the client in expressing feelings and opinions, but also gives a reality base for the probable response from the other party involved in the conflict. This can often remove the barrier that is keeping the client from making the decision and implementing the necessary action steps.

EXERCISE: DIALOGUING

Identify someone whom you constantly resent. Sitting in a chair, get in touch with all of the things the person does that you resent. Either verbally or in imagination, express your resentful feelings to this person. Now switch chairs. This time, think about what this person does that you appreci-

---

[11] Bohart, "Role Playing and Interpersonal Conflict Resolution," pp. 15–24.

ate. Identify your feelings of appreciation for this person. Now, verbally or in imagination, express all your feelings of appreciation to this person. Shuttle back and forth between the resentment and appreciation, switching chairs as you do so. After doing this, reflect on the experience. Did you feel that your feelings of resentment or appreciation seemed stronger or less intense than before you tried this? What can you now identify about yourself and about the other person?

If you would like to strengthen your feelings of appreciation for this person, try an extension of this dialogue during the next week:

1. Each time you notice you feel resentful of the person, switch chairs (in your head) so that you also experience the feelings of appreciation.
2. Whenever you are able to shift from resentment to appreciation, mark this down with a check mark on a card or a tally sheet.
3. At the end of the week, count your total number of tallies. If you were able to shift from resentment to appreciation, acknowledge yourself in some way—praise yourself or do something fun.
4. Reassess your relationship with this person, and contrast your feelings now with your feelings one week ago. What does this person do for you? How do you need this person?

Role Play as a Method of Behavior Change

The strategy of behavior rehearsal uses role play and practice attempts to help persons acquire new skills and to help persons behave more effectively under threatening or anxiety-producing conditions. Behavior rehearsal is used primarily in three instances:

1 The client does not have and needs to learn the necessary skills to handle a situation (*response acquisition*).
2. The client needs to learn to discriminate between positive and negative application of the skills or between inappropriate and appropriate times and places to use the skills (*response facilitation*).
3. The client's anxiety about the situation needs to be sufficiently reduced so that the client can use skills already learned, even though they are currently inhibited by anxiety (*response disinhibition*).

For example, if a client wants to increase self-disclosive behavior, but doesn't know what self-disclosure is or hasn't learned the skills involved in self-disclosing, the client has a deficient repertory in self-disclosure and needs to acquire certain skills (response acquisition). On the other hand, there are times when the skills already are in the client's repertoire, but the client needs clarification or discrimination training in when and how to employ the skills (response facilitation). We have all known persons who have self-disclosure skills but use the skills inappropriately. A person may self-disclose too much to someone who is disinterested and withhold personal information from a significant other. In another case, the client's anxiety perhaps has inhibited the skills (response disinhibition). In other words, a client may have learned the skills of appropriate self-disclosure but avoids self-disclosing because of anxiety the client feels in certain self-disclosive situations.

The "nuts and bolts" of behavior rehearsal consist of a series of graduated practice attempts in which the client rehearses the desired behaviors, starting with a situation that is manageable and is not likely to backfire. The rehearsal attempts may be arranged in a hierarchy according to level of difficulty or stress of different situations. Adequate practice of one situation is required before moving on to another scene. The practice of each scene should be very similar to the situations that occur in the client's environment. To simulate these situations realistically, use any necessary props and portray the other person involved with the client as accurately as possible. This portrayal should include acting out the probable response of this person to the client's new or different behavior.

Behavior rehearsal can be overt or covert. In covert behavior rehearsal, clients practice the target behavior by *imagining* themselves performing the response in certain situations. For instance, clients might imagine themselves successfully presenting an important speech or initiating a discussion with a friend or a boss. In overt rehearsal, the client *acts out* the target responses in role-played scenarios. Both covert and overt rehearsal seem to be quite effective.[12] Probably a client could benefit from engaging in both of these forms of behavioral rehearsal. Initially, the client might practice covertly and later act out the responses in role-played enactments. Covert rehearsal also can be used easily by clients as homework, since imaginary practice does not require the presence of another person.

Each scene should be practiced before moving on to the next scene. You can determine when a scene is rehearsed satisfactorily by three criteria proposed by Lazarus:

1. The client is able to enact the scene without feeling anxious.
2. The client's general demeanor supports the client's words.
3. The client's words and actions would seem fair and reasonable to an objective onlooker.[13]

However, the rehearsal efforts may be limited unless accompanied by some form of feedback or analysis of performance.

Feedback is an important part of role-play and rehearsal strategies. Feedback is a way for the client to recognize both the problems and successes encountered in the practice attempts. According to Melnick, feedback is a means of observing and evaluating one's performance and of initiating corrective action.[14] However, feedback should not be used indiscriminately.

[12] R. McFall and C. Twentyman, "Four Experiments in the Relative Contributions of Rehearsal, Modeling and Coaching to Assertion Training," *Journal of Abnormal Psychology* 81 (1973): 199–218.

[13] A. Lazarus, "Behavioral Rehearsal vs. Non-Directive Therapy vs. Advice in Effecting Behavior Change," *Behavior Research and Therapy* 4 (1966): 210.

[14] J. Melnick, "A Comparison of Replication Techniques in the Modification of Minimal Dating Behavior," *Journal of Abnormal Psychology* 81 (1973): 51–59.

Feedback may be more effective if the client is willing to change, if the feedback given is adequate but not overwhelming, and if the feedback helps the client identify other alternatives.[15]

Following rehearsal attempts, clients can be encouraged to evaluate their performances. You will be another important source of feedback. Remember to reinforce the client for gradual improvement. Feedback also can be supplied by videotaped and audiotaped playbacks of the client's practices. These taped playbacks may be more objective assessments of the client's performance. At first you can go over the tapes together and point out the strengths and limitations apparent in the practice. Gradually, the client should be able to analyze the taped playback alone—providing self-analysis and self-reinforcement for the practice efforts.

Modeling, Rehearsal, and Feedback: Components of Skill Training

It should be recognized that the strategies of modeling, rehearsal, and feedback can be combined as a skill-training package. These strategies often are used to teach clients problem-solving skills, decision-making skills, communication skills, and assertion skills. For example, in assertion training, you begin by having the client identify one situation in which he or she wants to be more assertive. Then specify what assertive behaviors are involved and what the client would like to say or do. The situation is modeled and role played consistently in the interview until the client can be assertive without experiencing any anxiety. Following successful completion of the task outside the interview, assertion training can continue for other kinds of situations involving self-assertion by the client. Successes at assertiveness will soon generalize to other situations as well; that is, it will become increasingly easier for clients to be assertive on their own without assistance and feedback.

As an illustration, suppose you are working with a student who reports a lack of assertive classroom behaviors. You and your client would first specify the desired assertive skills. You may need to observe the student in the classroom setting to identify these target behaviors. In counting the number of times the student engages in assertive classroom behavior (asking questions, voicing opinions, engaging in group discussion, giving reports, volunteering for blackboard work, initiating conversations with the teacher, etc.), you can obtain an accurate idea of the kind of assertive behaviors that are most prevalent in the client's repertoire and the ones the student needs most to strengthen. You can provide either live, symbolic, or covert models of these specific assertive behaviors. After the client has seen, listened to, read about, or imagined these modeled behaviors, the client can demonstrate and practice small steps of such assertive classroom behaviors in the interview. Following practice attempts in which the client is able to demonstrate repeated efforts of a given behavior within the

---

[15] W. J. McKeachie, "Psychology in America's Bicentennial Year," *American Psychologist* 31 (1976): 824.

interview, he or she should be encouraged to practice it on a daily basis in the classroom.

EXERCISE: BEHAVIOR REHEARSAL

With a partner, try out the process of behavior rehearsal. One of you should take the client's role and the other can assume the role of the helper. Have the client present a problem in which the desired change is to acquire a skill or to extinguish a fear. The counselor should try out the behavior rehearsal strategy to help the client meet this goal. Here are the things to remember to do:

1. Specify the target behavior(s).
2. Determine the situations in which the skills need to be used or the fear needs to be reduced.
3. Arrange these situations on a hierarchy, starting with the least difficult or least anxiety-producing situations and gradually moving up to situations of greater difficulty, complexity, or threat.
4. Beginning with the first situation on the hierarchy, have the client engage in covert rehearsal of the target response(s). Following this practice attempt, ask the client to analyze it.
5. Using the same situation, have the client engage in a role-play (overt) rehearsal. Give the client feedback about the strengths and limitations of this practice. Supplement your feedback with an audiotape or videotape analysis, if feasible.
6. Determine when the client has satisfactorily demonstrated the target skills or reduced anxiety within the interview rehearsals. Assign homework consisting of in vivo rehearsal of this one situation.
7. Repeat steps 4 through 6 for the other situations on the hierarchy.

COGNITIVE CHANGE

There is an increasing realization that client problems can be the result of client thoughts, attitudes, and beliefs. For instance, depression and anxiety seem to have cognitive components; persons who feel depressed or anxious may report a high incidence of self-defeating thoughts. Many clients will avoid engaging in desirable behaviors because of the kind of consequences they imagine will result from such action. Dealing with clients' thoughts about particular actions often reveals that they have certain fears about the outcomes. Usually these are fears such as, "I might be rejected"; "I might make a mistake"; or "Someone might not approve of what I did." More often than not, these fears are highly irrational, stimulated by a pattern of self-perpetuating, illogical thinking.

Since the inception of Ellis's rational-emotive therapy in 1962, there has been a surge of interest in counseling strategies that might effectively deal with client cognitive-related concerns such as those expressed in the examples above. Such strategies may be referred to as *cognitive therapy*,[16] *cognitive relabeling*,[17] or *cognitive behavior modification*.[18]

In some cases, a cognitive change strategy will be used as a primary helping method, as is the case when a person reports an excess of negative self-thoughts or when a client's anxiety is produced and maintained by worry-oriented thoughts and ideas. In other instances, cognitive change strategies may supplement other strategies in the total helping program. In working with persons who want to reduce behavioral excesses, such as smoking, drinking, or eating, a counselor might also need to help clients "clean up" their thoughts about these excessive behaviors. We now know, for example, that an important part of a therapeutic weight-control program involves helping obese clients overcome negative thinking about their weight and their treatment program, as well as about occasional relapses or eating binges.[19] Even terminally ill cancer patients seem to benefit from therapeutic strategies that strengthen their belief in their bodies ability to fight back.[20]

We shall describe two cognitive change strategies that can be used whenever negative or self-defeating thoughts are part of the client's reported concerns. These two strategies, *thought stopping* and *cognitive restructuring*, share a common purpose: to help people prevent irrational thoughts or illogical belief systems from interfering with effective functioning.

Thought Stopping

Often clients may be aware of engaging in self-defeating or illogical thinking, but continue to do so. In such cases, a therapeutic strategy that helps to control or eliminate these negative ideas is desirable. Thought stopping may be used whenever clients *constantly* ruminate on past, present, or future problems, or whenever clients continually engage in illogical or worry-oriented thinking.

Here is the way thought stopping usually proceeds: First, clients are instructed to imagine themselves involved in a situation that produces the irrational thought sequence. They are asked to verbalize the thoughts that are occurring as they imagine the scene. As soon as an illogical thought (one that is self-defeating and based on unrealistic fears and assumptions) is emitted, the thought is sharply interrupted by the counselor, who firmly

[16] A. T. Beck, *Cognitive Therapy and the Emotional Disorders* (New York: International University Press, 1976).

[17] M. R. Goldfried and G. C. Davison, *Clinical Behavior Therapy* (New York: Holt, Rinehart & Winston, 1976), pp. 158–85.

[18] M. Mahoney, *Cognition and Behavior Modification* (Cambridge, Mass.: Ballinger, 1974); D. Meichenbaum, *Cognitive-Behavior Modification: An Integrative Approach* (New York: Plenum, 1977).

[19] K. Mahoney and M. Mahoney, "*Cognitive Factors in Weight Reduction*," in *Counseling Methods*, ed. J. D. Krumboltz and C. E. Thoresen (New York: Holt, Rinehart & Winston, 1976), pp. 99–105.

[20] O. C. Simonton and S. S. Simonton, "Belief Systems and Management of the Emotional Aspects of Malignancy," *Journal of Transpersonal Psychology* 7 (1975): 29–47.

intervenes with the word "STOP!" Following this command, the client is instructed in ways of changing the thought pattern. For instance, you might suggest that the client shift to assertive thoughts, or focus on neutral events, or imagine pleasure-producing scenes. This same process is repeated with the visualization of different situations until the client can easily change the direction of his or her thoughts on command.

After this technique is demonstrated and practiced within the interview setting, the client is asked to continue using it with reference to the same situation outside the interview on a daily basis. For example, when clients continually ruminate about past mistakes, they can instruct themselves to stop, then change the thought and concentrate instead on a present-oriented situation. After one situation has been mastered, you and your client can use the same procedure to stop other illogical thoughts. For example, a client may worry about being wrong. You can help stop this thought and have the client concentrate instead on thinking about being right.

EXERCISE: THOUGHT STOPPING

Try thought stopping with a partner:

1. Have the other person identify some ruminative, nonproductive thinking in which he or she engages.
2. Ask the person to verbalize aloud his or her typical chain of thoughts.
3. As the person starts to ruminate or starts to verbalize nonproductive thinking, interrupt the person with a loud "STOP!" accompanied by a handclap.
4. Ask the person to describe what happened when you interrupted the chain of thinking.
5. Have the person do steps 2 and 3 again. This time instruct the person to interrupt the process, first overtly with a verbalized "Stop!" and then covertly with an imagined "Stop!"
6. Instruct the person to continue to apply the covert interruption to the thoughts as they occur during the week.

Cognitive Restructuring

Cognitive or rational restructuring involves not only helping clients learn to recognize and stop self-defeating thoughts, but to substitute these thoughts with positive, self-enhancing, or coping thoughts. The first part of cognitive restructuring parallels the thought-stopping strategy: Clients learn to stop obsessive, illogical, or negative thoughts as they occur. This involves discrimination training in which they are made aware of what "they tell themselves" before, during, and after problem situations. Clients might be instructed to note and record their negative thoughts before, during, and after stressful or depressing situations for one or two weeks.

After they are aware of the nature and types of their self-defeating thoughts, the counselor helps them work toward identifying more positive or coping thoughts that can replace the negative ones. These coping thoughts are considered to be incompatible with the self-defeating thoughts. It is best to tailor-make these coping thoughts for each client. Clients also need to learn coping thoughts to use before, during, and after problem situations. For example, a client who "blows" tests due to anxiety might concentrate on thoughts such as "I will be calm" or "Keep your mind on your studies" before an exam. During an exam, clients learn to concentrate on the exam and to stay calm instead of worrying about flunking or thinking about their nervousness. After using some coping thoughts, clients can be taught to reward or congratulate themselves for coping—instead of punishing themselves for worrying.

When clients have identified some possible alternative, coping thoughts to use, they can practice applying these thoughts through overt (role-play) and covert (imaginary) rehearsal. Identifying and internalizing coping thoughts seems to be crucial in order for clients to really benefit from cognitive restructuring. As Meichenbaum asserts, "it appears that the awareness of one's self-statements is a necessary but *not* sufficient condition to cause behavior change. One needs to produce incompatible self-instructions and incompatible behaviors."[21] Gradually, clients should be able to apply their newly found coping skills to the in vivo situations as these occur. If thought stopping and cognitive restructuring are successful, clients can detect increased use of coping thoughts and decreased level of stress in their actual environment.

EXERCISE: COGNITIVE RESTRUCTURING

This exercise is an opportunity for you to apply cognitive restructuring with yourself:

1. Think of a situation in which your performance is affected because of your thoughts about the situation.
2. Become aware of the nature of these thoughts. Keep a log of these thoughts that occur before, during, and after the situation for a week.
3. Analyze your log. Which of your thoughts are self-defeating or are not based on fact? Do your negative thoughts seem to occur mostly before, during, or after the situation?
4. Construct some coping thoughts to use at these problem times. The coping thoughts should help you focus on the task and stay calm.
5. Practice using these coping thoughts with imagery and role-play practices of the problem situation. Internalize these thoughts during your practice attempts.
6. As you feel comfortable with these practices, gradually apply the coping thoughts in the actual situation. You can use thought stopping to terminate the self-defeating thoughts and cognitive restructuring to replace these with coping thoughts.

[21] D. Meichenbaum, *Therapist Manual for Cognitive Behavior Modification* (Unpublished manuscript, University of Waterloo, Ontario, Canada, 1974), p. 51.

SELF-MANAGEMENT

Many persons are legitimately concerned about the long-term effects of helping. In an effort to promote enduring client changes, counselors have become more concerned with client self-directed change. This interest has led many counseling researchers and practitioners to explore the usefulness of a variety of helping strategies called *self-control*,[22] *self-regulation*,[23] or *self-management*.[24]

The primary characteristic of a self-management strategy is that the client administers the strategy and directs the change efforts with minimal assistance from the counselor. Self-management strategies are very useful in dealing with a number of client problems and may promote generalization to life settings of what clients learn in the interview. Self-management strategies are among the best strategies designed to strengthen client investment in the helping process. Self-management may eliminate the counselor as a "middle" person and ensure greater chances of client success because of the investment made by the client in the strategies for change. Three of the most useful self-management strategies include self-monitoring, self-reward, and self-contracting.

Self-Monitoring

Recent emphases in behavioral approaches suggest the efficacy of a number of self-control procedures, of which self-monitoring is the primary one. Self-monitoring involves having clients count and/or regulate given habits, thoughts, or feelings. Self-monitoring seems to interfere with the learned habit by breaking the stimulus-response association and by encouraging performance of the desired response—which is then often reinforced by the individual's sense of progress following its accomplishment.

There are two issues that affect the self-monitoring strategy—reactivity and reliability. *Reactivity* means that the process of noticing one's own behavior closely can cause the behavior to change. *Reliability* refers to the accuracy with which the client counts the behavior. For therapy purposes, you and your client should attempt to structure the self-monitoring in a way that maximizes the reactivity. Therefore, in implementing the procedure, you will need to consider what, how, and when to self-monitor.

What to monitor. An initial step involves selection of the behavior to monitor. Usually individuals will achieve better results with self-monitoring if they start by counting only one behavior—at least initially. Clients may, for example, count positive feelings about themselves or thoughts

[22] J. R. Cautela, "Behavior Therapy and Self-Control: Technique and Implications," in *Behavior Therapy: Appraisal and Status*, ed. C. Franks (New York: McGraw-Hill, 1969), pp. 323–40.

[23] F. H. Kanfer, "Self-Regulation: Research, Issues, and Speculation," in *Behavior Modification in Clinical Psychology*, ed. C. Neuringer and J. Michaels (New York: Appleton-Century-Crofts, 1970), pp. 178–220.

[24] M. J. Mahoney, "The Self-Management of Covert Behavior: A Case Study," *Behavior Therapy* 2 (1971): 575–78.

of competency. The counting encourages greater frequency of these kinds of thoughts and feelings. Clients may count the number of times they tell themselves to do well on a task, or they may count the number of behaviors related to goal achievement (the number of times they tell their spouse "I love you," the number of times they initiate conversations or participate in class discusssions, and so forth). The important thing is that they monitor behaviors that they value and care to change. If a client wishes to stop smoking, self-monitoring of this behavior could be very useful. Simply asking a person who doesn't wish to give up smoking to monitor this habit is not likely to be too effective.[25]

How to monitor. The particular method the client uses to count the target response will depend on the nature of the selected response. Generally, clients will count either the *frequency* or *duration* of a response. If they are interested in knowing how often the response occurs, they can use a frequency count to note the number of times they smoke, talk on the telephone, initiate social conversations, or think about themselves positively. Sometimes it is more useful to know the amount of time the behavior occurs. A person can count the duration or length of a behavior in these cases. For example, clients might count how long they studied, how long they talked on the telephone, or the length of depressed periods of thought. Occasionally, clients may find it useful to record both the frequency and duration of a response. In choosing to count the occurrences of a behavior either by the number or by the amount of time, there is a simple rule of thumb recommended by Watson and Tharp:

> If it is easy to count the number of separate times you perform the target behavior, count that. If it is not easy, or if the target behavior runs on for several minutes at a time, count the amount of time you do it.[26]

In some cases where the target response occurs very often or almost continuously, or when the onset and termination of the target responses are hard to detect, the frequency and duration methods of recording may not be too useful. In these instances, clients could record with an interval method. In the interval method of recording, they could divide the time for recording (8:00 A.M. to 8:00 P.M.) into time intervals such as thirty minutes, one hour, or two hours. During each time interval, they simply record the presence or absence of the behavior with a "yes" if the behavior occurred or a "no" if it did not. Mahoney and Thoresen refer to this as the *all-or-none* recording method.[27] Ciminero, Nelson, and Lipinski suggest the information gleaned by the all-or-none interval recording method may be increased if clients are instructed to rate each interval using a number

---

[25] R. M. McFall, "Effects of Self-Monitoring on Normal Smoking Behavior," *Journal of Consulting and Clinical Psychology* 35 (1970): 135–42.

[26] D. Watson and R. Tharp, *Self-Directed Behavior Change: Self-Modification for Personal Adjustment* (Monterey, Calif.: Brooks/Cole, 1972), p. 82.

[27] M. Mahoney and C. Thoresen, eds., *Self-Control: Power to the Person* (Monterey, Calif: Brooks/Cole, 1974).

system to indicate how often the target response occurred.[28] For example, using a five-point scale, persons could rate the occurrence of a response as a "0," "1," "2," "3," or "4" depending on whether the response occurred "never," "occasionally," "often," "very frequently," or "always."

Clients will need to record with the assistance of some device for recording. These can range from simple devices such as notecards, logs, and diaries for written recordings, to more mechanical devices such as a golf wrist counter, a kitchen timer, wristwatch, or a tape recorder. The device may increase the reactivity of self-monitoring if it is obtrusive;[29] yet it should not be so noticeable that it is embarrassing or awkward for clients to use. The device should be simple to use, convenient, portable, and economical.

When to record. The timing of self-monitoring can influence the change produced by this strategy. Generally, there are two times when clients can record: before the response (prebehavior monitoring) or after the response (postbehavior monitoring).[30] If the clients wish to use self-monitoring to decrease a response, prebehavior monitoring may be most effective; postbehavior monitoring may be more helpful when the goal is to increase a behavior. The rule of thumb for the timing of self-monitoring can be stated to clients as follows:

1. *To decrease the monitored behavior*: Since you want to decrease the number of cigarettes you smoke (or the number of self-critical thoughts you have), each time you have the urge to smoke but don't (or start to criticize yourself but refrain from doing so), then count this on your log.
2. *To increase a behavior*: Since you want to increase the number of times you verbally express your opinions to someone else (or the number of positive, self-enhancing thoughts), count and record on your log immediately after you express an opinion (or as soon as you are aware of thinking something positive about yourself or your accomplishments).

Counting, or quantifying, behaviors is the initial step in self-monitoring. The second and equally important step in self-monitoring is charting or plotting the behavior counts over a period of time. This permits clients to see progress that might not otherwise be apparent. It also permits clients to set daily goals that are more attainable than the overall goal. Clients can take weekly cumulative counts of self-monitored behaviors and chart them on a simple line graph. After graphing the data, the public display of the graph may set the occasion for both self- and external reinforcement.

[28] A. Ciminero, R. Nelson, and D. Lipinski, "Self-Monitoring Procedures," in *Handbook of Behavioral Assessment*, ed. A. Ciminero, K. Calhoun, and H. Adams (New York: Wiley, 1977), p. 199.
[29] R. Nelson, D. Lipinski, and R. Boykin, "The Effects of Self-Recorders' Training and the Obtrusiveness of the Self-Recording Device on the Accuracy and Reactivity of Self-Monitoring," *Behavior Therapy* 9 (1978): 200–208.
[30] A. Bellack, R. Rozensky, and J. Schwartz, "A Comparison of Two Forms of Self-Monitoring in a Behavioral Weight Reduction Program," *Behavior Therapy* 5 (1974): 523–30.

To summarize, self-monitoring is most likely to produce desired behavioral changes when the following conditions exist:

1. The client is motivated to change the behavior to be monitored.
2. The client monitors a limited number of behaviors and these behaviors are discrete.
3. The monitoring act is closely related in time prior to or after the monitored behavior.
4. The client receives some feedback from the monitoring that is compared with the client's goals.[31]

Self-Reward

Research suggests that the effects produced by self-monitoring may be greater and more permanent if self-monitoring is accompanied by other therapeutic strategies, such as self-reward, self-punishment, and self-contracting.[32] Self-monitoring can always be combined with other helping strategies as a way to collect data concerning the occurrence of goal behaviors. As we noted in the previous section, self-monitoring also can be used intentionally to induce therapeutic change. However, the therapeutic gains from self-monitoring may be maximized with the explicit use of other self-management strategies to increase or decrease a response.

Self-reward involves the self-presentation of rewards following the occurrence of a desired behavior. Self-reward is intended to strengthen a behavior. It is assumed that self-reward functions like external reinforcement. A *reinforcer* is something that, when administered following a target response, tends to maintain or increase the probability of that response in the future.

There are two ways clients can use self-reward. First, they can give themselves rewards after engaging in specified behaviors. For example, clients could imagine being on a sailboat after doing daily exercises or could buy themselves treats after daily studying. Or they could remove something negative after performing the desired behaviors. For instance, an overweight client could remove a "fat picture" from the wall after losing a certain number of pounds. In most cases we recommend the first approach (self-presentation of a positive stimulus) because it is more positive than the second. The first approach, which may be referred to as positive self-reward, has been validated by more research studies than the negative procedure.[33]

There are three major factors involved in helping a client use a self-reward strategy: what to use as rewards, how to administer the rewards, and when to administer the rewards.

---

[31] R. McFall, "Parameters of Self-Monitoring," in *Behavioral Self-Management: Strategies, Techniques, and Outcomes*, ed. R. Stuart (New York: Brunner/Mazel, 1977), pp. 196–214.

[32] M. Mahoney, N. Moura, and T. Wade, "The Relative Efficacy of Self-Reward, Self-Punishment, and Self-Monitoring Techniques for Weight Loss," *Journal of Consulting and Clinical Psychology* 40 (1973): 404–7.

[33] Ibid.

Types of rewards. First, you will want to help your clients select appropriate rewards. Clients should choose things that are truly reinforcing. There are different types of rewards to use. An example of a verbal-symbolic reward is self-praise, such as thinking, "I really did that well." Imaginal rewards involve visualizing or fantasizing scenes that produce pleasure and satisfaction. Material rewards include tangible events such as an enjoyable activity, a purchase, or tokens or points that can be exchanged for something. Rewards also can be current or potential. A current reward is something enjoyable that occurs on a daily basis, such as eating, reading, or getting the mail. A potential reward is something that could occur in the future which would be satisfying and enjoyable. Taking a trip and going out for a gourmet meal are examples of potential rewards.

Clients should be encouraged to select a variety of rewards, including both current and potential, material, imaginal, and verbal-symbolic. This may prevent one reward from losing its potency or impact. You can help clients select rewards by having them identify some ongoing and potentially satisfying thoughts and activities. An occasional client may have difficulty in identifying rewards. In lieu of using a very enjoyable activity as a reward, this client might choose a more mundane daily activity, such as answering the telephone or walking up or down stairs.

Using a frequently occurring activity as a reward is based on the *Premack principle*, which states that a high probability behavior can be used to reinforce a low probability behavior.[34] For instance, something a student engages in frequently, such as getting up from the desk, can be made contingent on something the student does infrequently, such as completing assignments or work problems. The rewards used can be tailored to each client, since not all events or fantasies are reinforcing for all persons. The selected rewards should relate to the client's personal history, be acceptable to the client, and be something the client wants to do and is capable of doing.[35]

Delivery of rewards. After selecting rewards, clients will need to work out ways to administer the rewards. They should know what has to be done in order to present themselves with a reward. You might encourage them to reward themselves for *gradual* progress toward the desired goal. Daily rewards for small steps are more effective than one delayed reward for a great improvement.

Timing of rewards. Clients also need to present the rewards at certain times in order to maximize the self-reward strategy. The reward should come only *after* target behavior has been performed in order to have the most impact.[36]

[34] D. Premack, "Reinforcement Theory," in *Nebraska Symposium on Motivation*, ed. D. Levin (Lincoln: University of Nebraska Press, 1965), pp. 123–80.

[35] F. H. Kanfer, "Self-Management Methods," in *Helping People Change*, ed. F. H. Kanfer and A. P. Goldstein (New York: Pergamon, 1975), p. 338.

[36] L. Homme et al., *How to Use Contingency Contracting in the Classroom* (Champaign, Ill.: Research Press, 1969).

Sometimes self-reward is used in conjunction with another self-management strategy: self-contracting.

Self-Contracting

Clients who are able to identify and own their behaviors often acknowledge that their current actions result in some undesirable consequences. They state how they would like the consequences to be different (goals). They may or may not realize that in order to change the consequences they must first modify the behaviors producing them. Behavior change of any kind can be a slow painful process requiring much time and effort on the client's part. Therefore, getting clients to make behavior changes is not easy. You must first obtain the client's *commitment* to change. A technique beneficial in gaining the cooperation and commitment of the client is *self-contracting*. The self-contract, which should be written, specifies what actions the client agrees to take in order to reach the desired goal. Furthermore, it contains a description of the conditions surrounding the action steps: *where* the client will undertake such actions, *how* (in what manner) the client will carry out the actions, and *when* (by what time) the tasks will be completed. These contract terms are specified by the client.

Self-contracts often are more successful when they are accompanied by self-reward. In other words, clients are more likely to commit themselves to a contract if they know there will be some kind of reward resulting from achievement of the contract terms. Encourage clients to provide their own reinforcements. The reward is made contingent upon successful completion of the contract; that is, the client must successfully complete the contract terms before engaging in the selected reward.

In some cases, a self-contract also may include sanctions that the client administers for failure to meet the contract terms. However, the rewards and sanctions should be balanced, and a self-contract that emphasizes positive terms may be more effective. The client will be more likely to adhere to the contract terms if the terms maximize the rewards for the person. The rewards also should be prearranged, so that the client obtains reinforcement for small gains. You can help clients develop contracts that specify behaviors that are within their capability and that provide reinforcement for gradual improvements.

Client Commitment to Self-Management

A critical problem in the effective use of any self-management strategy is having the client use the strategy regularly and consistently. There is some evidence that people who benefit from self-management use self-management strategies on a very consistent basis.[37]

Clients may be more likely to carry out self-management programs given the presence of certain conditions:

[37] M. G. Perri and C. S. Richards, "An Investigation of Naturally Occurring Episodes of Self-Controlled Behaviors," *Journal of Counseling Psychology* 24 (1977): 178–83.

1. The use of the self-management program will provide enough advantages or positive consequences to be worth the cost to the client in terms of time and effort. The self-management program must do more than simply meet the status quo.
2. The client's use of the program may be strengthened by enlisting the support and assistance of other persons—as long as their roles are positive, not punishing. Former clients, peers, or friends can aid the client in achieving the goals through reinforcement of the client's regular use of the self-management strategies.
3. The counselor maintains some minimal contact with the client during the time the self-management program is being carried out. Counselor reinforcement is quite important in successful implementation of self-management efforts.

You can provide reinforcement (anything that serves to increase the frequency of a desired response) easily through oral approval ("That's great"; "I like that") or by knowledge of progress ("You did very well"; "You did the task perfectly"; "You've done a great job in improving your study habits"). Have the client drop in or telephone during the course of the self-management program. This enables you to provide immediate encouragement to the client.

EXERCISE: SELF-MANAGEMENT

This exercise is designed to help you modify some aspect of your helping behavior with the use of a self-management program.

1. Select and define a behavior you wish to increase or decrease that, when changed, will make you a better helper. The behavior may be an overt one, such as using more silence or asking open questions instead of closed questions. Or the behavior may be covert, such as reducing the number of apprehensive thoughts about seeing clients or increasing some self-enhancing thoughts about your helping potential.
2. Self-record the occurrence of the behavior for a week or two to obtain a baseline measure. The baseline gives you the present level of the behavior before applying any self-management strategies.
3. After obtaining some baseline data, deliberately try to increase or decrease the behavior (depending on your goal) using self-monitoring. (Remember that prebehavior monitoring is used to decrease a response; and postbehavior monitoring is used to increase a response.) Do this for about two weeks. Does the behavior change over time in the desired direction? If so, you may want to continue with self-monitoring for a few more weeks. Charting and posting of the data will help you see visible progress.
4. You may want to augment any behavior change produced by self-monitoring with either self-reward or self-contracting. Work out a self-reward plan or write out a self-contract.
5. Continue to self-record the occurrence of the behavior; then compare these data with the data you gathered during baseline (step 2). What changes occurred?
6. How did your use of self-management affect this helping behavior?

EXERCISE: INTERVENTION STRATEGIES

In this exercise, three hypothetical client cases are described. The first case is used as an example. We describe the client's probable goals and the intervention strategies we would use to help this client reach these goals. After reading over the example, work through the other cases in a similar manner. You can do this activity alone, with a partner, or in a small group discussion. You may wish to exchange your responses and ideas with other helpers or share your thoughts with your instructor.

Case 1

Sally is a college freshman at a large university; she is overwhelmed by the size of the university, having lived in a small town all her life. She is concerned about her shyness and feels it is preventing her from making friends. She reports being uncertain about how to reach out to people. She is concerned about her performance on tests. Although she believes her study habits are adequate, she reports that she "blows" the tests because she gets so uptight about them.

PROBABLE COUNSELING GOALS

1. To help Sally identify and acquire the social skills involved in initiating and maintaining friendships
2. To help Sally reduce her anxiety about tests

POSSIBLE COUNSELING STRATEGIES

1. For goal 1, Sally is concerned about identifying and acquiring some social skills. Because she is uncertain about the skills necessary for making friends, we would first use a modeling strategy (either live, symbolic, or covert) in which Sally saw some models demonstrate some ways to initiate and maintain friendships. To help Sally actually acquire these skills, we would employ role play, rehearsal, and feedback. This would give Sally an opportunity to practice the modeled skills under low-threat conditions and to refine these skills with objective feedback. Finally, once Sally has demonstrated these skills in the interview role plays, we might suggest that she use self-monitoring to strengthen her actual use of the skills in vivo. For instance, Sally could self-monitor such things as the number of times she initiates a conversation, the times she asks a friend to accompany her somewhere, the amount of time she talks to friends, and so forth.
2. For goal 2, Sally is concerned about trying to reduce her uptight feelings about tests. We would first try a combination of thought stopping and cognitive restructuring. We would spend some time helping Sally identify the possible things she is thinking before and during tests, and show her how any self-defeating thoughts could detract from her concentration and impair her performance. We would teach Sally how to stop these thoughts with thought stopping, and then use cognitive restructuring to help her identify and practice alternative coping thoughts. As she becomes able to do this in actual test-taking situations, she could also self-monitor the times she stopped the anxiety-producing thoughts and the times she was able to concentrate on coping thoughts.

Case 2

Mr. and Mrs. Yule have been married for two years. Both are in their sixties, and this is their second marriage; their previous spouses had died within the last ten years. Mr. and Mrs. Yule are concerned that they rushed into this second relationship without adequate thought. They report that they argue constantly about everything. They feel they have forgotten how to talk to each other in a civil manner. Mrs. Yule states that she realizes her constant nagging upsets Mr. Yule; Mr. Yule discloses that his spending a lot of time with his male buddies irritates Mrs. Yule.

PROBABLE COUNSELING GOALS

1. _____

   _____

2. _____

   _____

POSSIBLE COUNSELING STRATEGIES

1. _____

   _____

   _____

   _____

   _____

2. _____

   _____

   _____

   _____

   _____

Case 3

Arthur is a third-grader at Malcolm Elementary School. Arthur is constantly getting into trouble for a number of things. Arthur admits that he starts a lot of fights with the other boys. He says he doesn't know why or how, but suddenly he is punching at them. Only after these fights does he realize his anger got out of hand. Arthur realizes his behavior is causing some of the kids to avoid him, yet he believes he would like their friendship. He is not sure how to handle his temper so that he doesn't lash out at his peers.

PROBABLE COUNSELING GOALS

1. _____

2. _____

POSSIBLE COUNSELING STRATEGIES

1. _____

   _____

   _____

   _____

   _____

   _____

2. _____

   _____

   _____

   _____

   _____

   _____

SUMMARY

In working with clients, all of whom present unique concerns and circumstances, you may find great use for the strategies described in this chapter. However, there are several cautions to consider in trying to use a counseling strategy effectively. The first caution in strategy implementation is to avoid oversimplification of the procedure. Although a procedure may seem relatively simple to implement, even with little experience, any therapeutic endeavor can be for "better or worse" depending on how it is administered. Second, you must practice using strategies. Like all skills, they will not be as effective when you first start using them, but your skill will grow as you practice. Finally, keep in mind that counselilng is likely to be most effective when a number of these strategies are used in conjunction with one another and when the underlying counselor-client relationship contains a high level of respect and trust.

RECOMMENDED READINGS

CORMIER, WILLIAM H., and L. SHERILYN CORMIER, *Interviewing Strategies for Helpers: Fundamental Skills and Cognitive Behavioral Interventions.* 2d ed. Monterey, Calif.: Brooks/Cole, 1985.

Cormier and Cormier provide eight chapters of therapeutic interventions for the counselor to examine and rehearse. These include symbolic modeling, emotive imagery, meditation and muscle relaxation, systematic desensitization, self management approaches, and strategies for managing client resistance.

GOLDFRIED, M. R., and G. C. DAVISON, *Clinical Behavior Therapy*. New York: Holt, Rinehart & Winston, 1976.

The authors describe and illustrate the use of various helping strategies within a behaviorally oriented therapeutic relationship.

KANFER, F. H., and A. P. GOLDSTEIN, eds., *Helping People Change*. New York: Pergamon, 1975.

A number of different authors have written excellent articles in this edited book dealing with such topics as cognitive change, self-management, modeling, and role play.

KRUMBOLTZ, J. D., and C. E. THORESEN, eds., *Counseling Methods*. New York: Holt, Rinehart & Winston, 1976.

This book includes well-illustrated applications of therapeutic strategies for such problems as behavioral deficits, behavioral excesses, decision-making problems, and physical problems. A diagnostic Table of Contents is also included for an easy reference of various strategies and different client problems.

SCHWARTZ, A., and I. GOLDIAMOND, *Social Casework: A Behavioral Approach*. New York: Columbia University Press, 1975.

The authors use two extended-case examples to show how various therapeutic programs are applied to treat client problems.

SHELTON, J. L., and J. M. ACKERMAN, *Homework in Counseling and Psychotherapy*. Springfield, Ill.: Charles C Thomas, 1974.

The authors describe a number of action plans designed to deal with such problems as anxiety, depression, aggressiveness, nonassertiveness, and marital discord.

CHAPTER TWELVE

Receiving and Using Supervision

by Janine M. Bernard[*]

Thus far, this book has focused on the many facets of the relationship between the counselor and client and has outlined numerous ways to enhance that relationship. At this point, we shall discuss another essential relationship in the process of helping—the relationship between the supervisor and the counselor. Our discussion will not be complete because the supervision relationship has as many potential facets as the counseling relationship. Rather, this final chapter will provide a sketch of supervision parameters with the hope that it will help you to use supervision more quickly and more fully.

THE PARAMETERS OF SUPERVISION

In order to understand supervision, we need to consider what happens in supervision, who provides the supervision, and in what context supervision occurs. Different authors have highlighted different aspects of supervision in their definitions. Kutzik, for example, stressed the hierarchical relationship between supervisor and the supervisee when he defined *supervision* as "a continuous relationship—of an organizational superior and subordinate—supervisor and supervisee, respectively—in which the latter is required to report regularly to the former on the state of his or her work and the supervisor provides direction that the supervisee is bound to follow."[1] Hart emphasized the learning of the counselor in his definition:

[*] Janine M. Bernard, Ph.D., is Associate Professor and Director of the School, Agency, and Family Counseling Program at Fairfield University, Fairfield, Connecticut.
[1] Alfred J. Kutzik, "The Medical Field." In *Supervision, Consultation, and Staff Training in the Helping Professions*, ed. Florence W. Kaslow et al. (San Francisco: Jossey-Bass, 1977), p. 5.

"Clinical supervision is an ongoing educational process in which one person in the role of supervisor helps another person in the role of supervisee acquire appropriate professional behavior through an examination of the supervisee's professional activities."[2] Hess addressed the relationship between supervisor and supervisee when he defined supervision as "a relationship where one or more person's skills in conducting psychotherapy or mental health services are intentionally and potentially enhanced by the interaction with another person."[3] Finally, Aubrey added an important dimension in his definition of supervision by focusing on its end product, services to clients: "Supervision in its simplest and most direct connotation is an activity designed to guarantee that certain guidance and counseling goals and outcomes are accomplished."[4]

Based on these definitions, clinical supervision contains the following characteristics in some form:

1. One person of more developed ability and/or higher organizational status and one or more persons of lesser ability and/or lesser organizational status
2. A relationship/understanding/contract between supervisor and supervisee
3. A process that is aimed at the improvement of the supervisee's clinical performance
4. A responsibility (ethical and, in some instances, legal) on the part of the supervisor for the services delivered to the supervisee's clients (or future clients)
5. An assumption of either formal or informal monitoring of the supervisee's progress, including some form of evaluation

A complete definition of supervision requires that we turn our attention to the next two questions: Who is a supervisor? and, In what context does supervision occur? The obvious answer to the first of these questions is that anyone who engages in supervision is a supervisor. More specifically, a clinical supervisor can be a prepracticum or a practicum instructor, a doctoral student working with graduate student trainees, or a supervisor in a field setting who works with trainees as part of their graduate internship. Once a counselor has completed graduate training, the employer, supervisor, or senior counselor in an agency, school, or other work setting may be the clinical supervisor.

It probably should be noted that part of becoming a supervisor involves a *decision* to supervise. In graduate training, this decision is implicit, if not explicit, in the structure of the training program. The practicum instructor has made a decision to supervise by teaching the course. Later on, however, as counselors enter their first professional positions, supervision may or may not be forthcoming. In such a situation, it is often up to

---

[2] Gordon M. Hart, *The Process of Clinical Supervision* (Baltimore: University Park Press, 1982), p. 12.

[3] Allen K. Hess, *Psychotherapy Supervision: Theory, Research and Practice* (New York: Wiley, 1980), p. 528.

[4] Roger F. Aubrey, "Supervision of Counselors in Elementary and Secondary Schools," *Counselor Supervision* ed. John Boyd (Muncie, Ind.: Accelerated Development, 1978), p. 298.

the counselor to request supervision in order to stimulate a senior professional's decision to supervise.

This brings us to another important distinction, that between clinical supervision and administrative supervision. Your employer in a mental health center, for instance, is your administrative supervisor since this person has the power to hire and/or fire you, to increase your salary, to determine your job description, and so forth. However, this person is not automatically a clinical supervisor. A clinical supervisor must be working with you in some manner to improve your counseling ability. Therefore, even a peer could be a clinical supervisor, if that person has the ability to enhance your growth, and both of you have determined to enter into a supervisory relationship. (Many advanced professionals in private practice rely on a peer supervision model with their partners in order to avoid stagnation in their work.)

THE FOCUS OF SUPERVISION

What is it that my supervisor is looking for? For beginning counselors or counselors who are working with a new supervisor, this is a common and legitimate question. Obviously, good intentions are not enough to warrant the kind of feedback a counselor hopes to receive from a supervisor, because many counselors with the best of intentions have received less than accolades from their supervisors. This section will describe the four major areas that supervisors focus on when evaluating counselor performance. Understanding the differences among these categories will help you not only to know what it is your supervisor will be looking for in your counseling, but also to hear your supervisor's feedback with a more discriminating ear.

The four areas will be described as *skills* to imply that all four categories represent groups of behaviors that can be learned (to differing degrees for different people) and that can be refined. The four areas or categories are (1) process skills, (2) conceptualization skills, (3) personalization skills, and (4) professional skills.[5]

Process Skills

Process skills are those overt behaviors that distinguish counseling from other social interactions. They are what you *do* in your sessions. Process skills include all *observable* counselor behaviors; therefore, the other three categories must often be inferred from the counselor's process skills. Greeting the client, requesting information, reflecting what you hear, confronting what seems to be a contradiction, structuring a role play, supporting a client in distress—all are process skills. Process skills range from

[5] Janine M. Bernard, "Supervisor Training: A Discrimination Model," *Counselor Education and Supervision* 19 no. 1 (1979): 60–68; and Wayne Lanning, "Development of the Supervisor Emphasis Rating Form," *Counselor Education and Supervision* 25, (1986): 191–96.

simple (restatement) to sophisticated (parodoxical intervention) depending on the abilities of the counselor.

When a supervisor is focusing on a counselor's process skills, the feedback will sound something like this:

> "I thought your initial question was a good one."
>
> "You used a lot of questions in your session. I wonder if you could increase your use of reflections."
>
> "Would you be willing to try a role play with the client?"
>
> "Your nonverbal behavior communicated a lot of caring for the client."

Conceptualization Skills

As the term implies, conceptualization skills are thinking skills. Much of the covert activity of the counselor falls into this category. Conceptualization skills include identifying the major concern of the client, recognizing dominant themes in a counseling session, planning for future sessions, and choosing a particular helping response (or technique) with a certain goal in mind. Using a reflection of affect in a counseling session is a process skill; choosing which client message to reflect is a conceptualization skill. Without adequate conceptualization skills, process skills are relatively useless because the counselor's responses, even if well-executed, would be random or unrelated to what was happening in the session. Purposeful counseling occurs when the counselor conceptualizes accurately.

Supervisory statements that have as their focus the conceptualization skills of the counselor are as follows:

> "When you asked about her mother, what were you looking for?"
>
> "I thought you picked up all of the major themes in the session."
>
> "Where are you going from here with this client?"
>
> "Did that homework assignment accomplish what you hoped it would?"

Notice that three of the four examples of supervisor feedback were in the form of questions. This will often be the case for conceptualization skills and, similarly, for personalization skills. The supervisor can only infer what the counselor had in mind based on the process skills observed. In fact, the supervisor may not know where the counselor's skill deficit lies until such questions are answered. For example, the counselor may have asked a question when a reflection would have been far more helpful. But before the supervisor can be of help to the counselor, it must be determined whether the counselor (1) did not know how to phrase a helpful reflection (process skill deficit), or (2) did not know that a reflection was called for (conceptualization skill deficit).

Personalization Skills

The term *personalization skill* was originated to suggest that the counselor uses personal attributes, for better or for worse, in the therapeutic relationship.[6] The existence of such a category is an acknowledgment that counseling is indeed a very personal activity, and that it is impossible to separate our personal attributes and liabilities from our work entirely. Personalization also refers to the degree to which we have adapted to the role of helper. Therefore, personalization skills would include being comfortable with the professional responsibility of being a counselor, being able to separate your reactions to an issue from those of the client, allowing your sense of humor to emerge, not being defensive with an accusing client, being able to handle a range of emotions in yourself or when presented by the client, and being able to accept constructive criticism from your supervisor.

Possible supervisory comments that would address personalization skills are as follows:

"You were able to keep your composure, even when the client became agitated. That's good."

"It seemed to me that you almost apologized when giving the client a homework assignment, as if you didn't want to waste her time. That communicated a lack of confidence on your part. Is that how you felt?"

"When your client stated his opinions about working women with small children, I thought you stepped out of your counselor role and started arguing with him. I wondered if he was baiting you and if you did take the bait."

"You're awfully quiet whenever I give you my feedback about your last counseling session. I've been wondering what that means."

Professional Skills

Professional skills have as much to do with performance outside the counseling relationship as within.[7] Perhaps these skills are less noticeable in initial training experiences and more evident in later experiences. They can overlap with personalization skills (for example, being late for a counseling appointment because you are intimidated by the client), but remain a discreet category in and of themselves. These skills include turning in written reports on time, safeguarding confidentiality, behaving professionally in field placement, using others' professional titles when appropriate, dressing appropriately for counseling contacts, and related behaviors.

As you will note, some of the items listed here seem far more important than others. Safeguarding confidentiality is much more critical than not wearing jeans to see clients. On the other hand, what appears frivolous to some people may be very important to a client. If we remember that clients are in an extremely vulnerable position in asking for help, we might be more receptive to the idea that the environment within which that help is offered is intrinsically related to the help itself. For example, picture a client entering a counseling center to find three or four staff members

---

[6] Janine Bernard, "Supervisor Training."
[7] Wayne Lanning, "Supervisor Emphasis Rating Form."

laughing raucously. Assuming that the client is feeling somewhat ambivalent about seeking counseling, many negative thoughts could be stimulated by such a scene ("They're laughing about the client who just left"). Now assume that the counselor seeing this client is one of those jovial staff members. It is very unlikely that the counseling session that follows will be unrelated to the professional context that was presented to the client when he or she arrived.

Examples of supervisor comments that address professional skills are as follows:

> "This might sound picky, but I don't think you should chew gum while you are counseling this client."
>
> "I was pleased with how you handled the referral to the Family Counseling Center. Everything was in order."
>
> "The last report you turned in had some grammatical errors and the use of slang. I've noted them on the report and would like you to rewrite it."
>
> "What are you going to do if Elisabeth's teacher asks you about the content of your counseling with Elisabeth?"

Discriminating among Categories

Keeping the four categories in mind, it is important to realize that all four are present all the time in your work as a counselor. For example, as you begin a session with a new client, you will need process skills to proceed adequately; you will have thought about how you want the session to progress; you will be choosing your personal responses carefully; and you will be trying to present a professional appearance. Because all four areas are operating at all times, your supervisor is making some assumptions when choosing to focus on one category rather than the other three when giving you feedback. Perhaps an example will help make this point clearer.

In a recent supervision workshop, a videotape of a counseling session was shown in which the client teared up as she discussed a sensitive topic. When that happened, the counselor became very quiet and asked just one question for clarification. After the tape was viewed, a group of professional supervisors were asked to write down comments they would want to make to the counselor. Two of the supervisors focused on the segment of tape described above, but approached it from different angles. One said, "I wanted the counselor to say something to the client, to comfort her in some way." The other remarked, "I thought the counselor was threatened by the client's show of emotion. I would want to discuss this with her."

The first supervisor approached the issue as a process skill deficit (the counselor needed to do something that she did not do), and the second supervisor approached it as a personalization skill deficit (emotion may threaten this counselor). As you can see, the assumptions that were being made about the counselor were very different for the two supervisors.

In the situation just described, neither supervisor knew the counselor.

It could make a big difference how a supervisor evaluates counseling behavior by knowing the counselor's strengths and weaknesses. On the other hand, supervisors have their own biases when observing counseling sessions; some are more likely to see events in process terms, while others are more likely to see them in conceptual terms. It is important for counselors to have some idea of the choices available to supervisors so they can appreciate the assumptions that go with those choices.

For your own part, you can begin to evaluate your counseling sessions by asking four simple questions:

> Did I know what to do in the session?
> Did I know what I wanted to do?
> Was I comfortable at that point?
> Was my performance that of a professional counselor?

STYLES OF SUPERVISION

Now that you have a better idea of what supervisors look for in training and supervising counselors, let's turn our attention to the choices supervisors make about their own behavior. As you will soon discover, if you have not already, different supervisors have different styles. Sometimes their style makes you feel confident and supported, and sometimes their style has a less positive effect on you. At least some of this has to do with the role they choose as they work with you. By describing the different supervisory roles and their purposes, perhaps we can help you to further understand the supervision process and its potential outcomes. Perhaps we can also encourage dialogue between you and your supervisor if the role being used in your supervision is giving you problems.

The Role of Teacher

The most common role for supervisors during the initial training of counselors is the *teacher role*. (For purposes of clarification we shall use the word *instructor* to mean the person responsible for teaching a particular course, leaving the word *teacher* to mean a particular role or style the instructor may or may not wish to assume.) When in the teacher role, the supervisor takes responsibility for knowing what the counselor needs to do or learn. Therefore, the supervisor might instruct the counselor about a new technique, might model a new intervention, or might make other direct suggestions regarding the counselor's work. When the supervisor acknowledges the rightness or wrongness of a particular counselor strategy, the teacher role is being used. When a supervisor is in the teacher role, there is no question who is in charge.

Of the supervisor responses listed in the last section, several were in the teacher role. "Your nonverbal behavior communicated a lot of caring for the client," is an example of a supervisor in this role. The supervisor is taking full responsibility for knowing what is appropriate or inappropriate nonverbal behavior. Most instructional comments and evaluative comments are teacher comments.

The Role of Counselor

When supervisors focus on the interpersonal or intrapersonal dynamics of their counselors or trainees, they are most likely in the *counselor role*. The goal of the supervisor in this role is most often the personal growth of the counselor. Historically, this role has been widely used by supervisors, based on the assumption that the most legitimate way for counselors to grow professionally is to grow personally. Although the last two decades have offered differing opinions of this premise, there are times when the counselor role is the necessary and most desirable option for the supervisor to use. (It is important, however, for the supervisor to be careful to avoid a dual relationship and to suggest a referral to someone else if extensive counseling for personal issues is needed.)

Referring again to the supervisor statements listed earlier, the following is an example of a supervisor in the counselor role: "You're awfully quiet whenever I give you my feedback about your last counseling session. I've been wondering what that means." Another combined both teacher and counselor roles. See if you can identify the two roles in this comment: "It seemed to me that you almost apologized when giving your client a homework assignment, as if you didn't want to waste her time. That communicated a lack of confidence on your part. Is that how you felt?"

The Role of Consultant

When the goal of the supervisor is to encourage trainees to think on their own and to trust their own insights, the *consultant role* is most appropriate. When in this role, supervisors limit themselves to being a resource for their trainees. The authority for what will transpire in the trainee's counseling is more equally shared. As a result, the consultant role conveys a degree of mutual trust and professional respect not necessarily found in the other two roles. On the other hand, respect is the expectation that the counselor can and will put forth the effort to use this role suitably.

A consultant comment from the preceding section is: "Did that homework assignment accomplish what you hoped it would?" This is a consultant response because the supervisor is not telling the counselor that the assignment did or did not succeed. However, if the counselor answers "Yes," and the supervisor responds, "Well, I don't agree," then the supervisor has very quickly changed from a consultant role to a teacher role.

The Need for Different Roles

One well-documented model of supervision is the *developmental model*, which describes counselor growth as advancing through sequential skill levels.[8] Depending on the developmental level of the counselor, different supervisor roles may be warranted.

Research indicates that trainees prefer their supervisors to be in the teacher role initially.[9] This is because they are unsure of themselves, and the teacher role gives them the structure and sense of security that they need at first. After they have received considerable training, they are more likely to prefer a consultant approach. When the supervisor is in this role, it allows the counselors to stretch their wings before they assume full responsibility for their clientele. Throughout training and beyond, the counselor role may be needed (if not welcome) because trainees occasionally hit personal snags that block their therapeutic efforts.

Supervisors' roles can be deliberate or the result of personal preference or habit. Some supervisors are "born teachers" and have a difficult time altering their style, even when the situation calls for it. Other supervisors keep their identity as counselors foremost in their work and approach their trainees as they would approach their clients. Finally, some supervisors like to give all trainees the opportunity to go at their own pace and prefer the consultant role. Frequently, the use of role involves a trial-and-error process. If the consultant role doesn't work with one trainee, then the teacher role is tried, whether or not the supervisor is aware of this change.

In the example given at the end of the previous section, the supervisor switched from consultant to teacher when the consultant role did not produce the desired response. (The supervisor obviously wanted the trainee to say that the homework did not accomplish what had been hoped.) This was not a good use of the consultant role because the supervisor was not willing to go along with the trainee's judgment. A direct teacher statement, "I don't think the homework assignment worked as you had hoped," would have been better in the long run.

You might be asking, "What if I don't like my supervisor's style? What can I do about it?" First of all, you might see if you encourage a certain role behavior. For example, if you approach supervision by asking a lot of questions, you are inviting your supervisor to assume the teacher role. If you try to convince your supervisor that you felt very anxious in your last session, you are (perhaps inadvertently) requesting the counselor role. When you make definitive statements about your work, you are encouraging a consultant role from your supervisor.

---

[8] Brian W. McNeil, Cal D. Stoltenberg, and Richard A. Pierce, "Supervisees' Perceptions of their Development: A Test of the Counselor Complexity Model," *Journal of Counseling Psychology* 32 (1985): 630–633; and Cal Stoltenberg, "Approaching Supervision from a Developmental Perspective: The Counselor-complexity Model," *Journal of Counseling Psychology* 28 (1981): 59–65; and Everett L. Worthington, Jr., "Empirical Investigation of Supervision of Counselors as they Gain Experience," *Journal of Counseling Psychology* 31 (1984): 63–75; and Everett L. Worthington, Jr. and Avner Stern, "Effects of Supervisor and Supervisee Degree Level and Gender on the Supervisory Relationship," *Journal of Counseling Psychology* 32 (1985): 252–262.

[9] Frederic E. Rabinowitz, P. Paul Heppner, and Helen J. Roehlke, "Descriptive Study of Process and Outcome Variables of Supervision over Time, *Journal of Counseling Psychology* 33, (1986) 292–300; and Everett L. Worthington, Jr., and Helen J. Roehlke, "Effective Supervision as Perceived by Beginning Counselors-in-Training," *Journal of Counseling Psychology* 26, (1979): 64–73.

If you believe that the problem is not in your approach but due to your supervisor's preference, you can ask if another role might be tried for a while. Again, knowing about the supervision process allows you to influence it. You might want to have your supervisor in the consultant role rather than the teacher or counselor role. One counselor approached her supervisor with this request. Her supervisor's reaction was, "I think that's a good idea. I agree that I've been too active in supervision. On the other hand, if it's going to work, I think you need to come to supervision more prepared. Perhaps you could review your tapes [audiotapes of counseling sessions] ahead of time and be prepared to identify segments that gave you difficulty and give your opinion of what went wrong." The counselor found this a reasonable plan. You might have noticed that the supervisor was *teaching* the counselor how to use him as a *consultant*. This kind of transition is often needed when a change of supervision role is to occur.

As a final note, we would like to mention that many, if not most, supervisors use all three styles in their work. It is not necessary that you be able to track your supervisor's style at all times. Rather, the issue of supervision role becomes relevant when you are trying to pinpoint why you are feeling stressed under supervision, or why you don't think you are progressing as quickly as you would like. The supervisor's role may or may not be the problem, but it is one more important piece of the puzzle for you to consider.

METHODS OF SUPERVISION

Now that we have discussed the different foci in supervision and the different roles a supervisor can assume, we shall turn our attention to the methods available to supervisors to accomplish their work. Obviously, supervisors must have some way to gain access to the trainee's counseling if they are to influence it.

Self-report

Until the introduction of technology into most counselor training programs, the most frequent form of supervision was for the counselor to report to the supervisor, either in writing or verbally, what was transpiring in counseling, and for the supervisor to react to this information as presented. This method of supervision is called *self-report* because the counselor is in control of what he or she chooses to report about the counseling session or relationship. Self-reporting is still used in supervision, though not as frequently as it once was, and not as often in the initial stages of counselor training (prepracticum and practicum). When self-reporting is used, the focus is generally on conceptualization and personalization skills. A major disadvantage of self-reporting, and the reason for its decline in popularity, is that it does not allow the supervisor to help the counselor work on blind spots. Those supervisors who tend to prefer self-report are those who adhere theoretically to the assumption that the most salient aspect of supervision is the relationship between the supervisor and supervisee.

Audiotape, Videotape, and Live Observation

The use of audiotape, videotape, and live observation are combined here because they all involve a similar supervision approach, that of observing a trainee's counseling, followed by a critique of what was heard and seen. Most training programs prefer this form of supervision, at least in the beginning, and have some facility or laboratory for this purpose. The advantage of direct (live observation) or indirect (audio or videotape) observation is that it allows the supervisor to address the process skills that were apparent in the observed session. In addition, this method of supervision allows supervisors to compare their perceptions of what transpired in counseling with those of their counselors when the case is subsequently discussed.

Live Supervision

Live supervision is different from live observation in that the former includes the active participation of the supervisor during counseling. Because live supervision is in some ways a team approach to counseling, it is typically reserved for advanced trainees. When using live supervision, the supervisor observes the session behind a one-way mirror and interrupts the session to give the counselor a suggestion. There are several ways to structure this type of supervision: (1) supervisors can phone in their suggestions using a closed-circuit phone intercommunication system; (2) supervisors can call the counselor out of the counseling room to discuss the progress of the session; (3) there can be a prearranged time (for example, twenty minutes into the session) when the counselor will leave to discuss the session with the supervisor; or (4) counselors can wear a small hearing device in their ear (referred to as a "bug in the ear") so the supervisor can make comments without interrupting the session.

Although this method of supervision has been accused of interfering with the counselor/client relationship, it offers some distinct advantages. Because the supervisor is working closely with the counselor, difficult cases can be assigned to the trainee more quickly because, in effect, the trainee is not "alone" in the counseling room. In addition, the supervisor can redirect a session that is going poorly, rather than waiting until later to give the counselor remedial feedback. As a result, there is more opportunity for success from the trainee's standpoint. To date, those supervisors and counselors using live supervision have found it to be a very satisfactory method of training and of accomplishing the goals of supervision.

Simulation

Not all supervision involves actual clients. Especially in the earlier phases of training, trainees may be asked to role play different counseling situations in order to gain some experience prior to taking on the responsibility of seeing actual clients. When simulating, trainees are asked either to share a real concern for the purpose of training, or are given a role to play with which they may or may not have had any life experience. Simulation can be used in conjunction with any of the methods of supervision described above.

Individual versus Group Supervision

Finally, we should mention that supervision can occur individually, one supervisor with one counselor, or in a group of counselors. Typically, the trainee will receive some of both forms during a counselor education program. In individual supervision, the focus will be on the trainee exclusively, with the supervisor offering his or her expertise when they confer about the progress being made by different clients and the trainee's own growth. In a group, trainees usually take turns presenting one of their cases, and the group then discusses it. There is potentially more opportunity for different instructional techniques with group supervision, including role plays (with feedback from the observers) for the purpose of practicing different approaches. Group supervision also allows the advantages of permitting trainees to learn from the cases of their peers as well as their own cases.

AVOIDING SUPERVISION

At this point, we would like to reiterate that because counseling is a very personal activity, feedback about your counseling can be taken very personally, leaving you feeling highly anxious and threatened by the prospect of receiving supervision. It can be difficult to separate your value as a person from your success as a helper when your motivation to help is strong. Therefore, we would like to address the issue of avoiding supervision. Most counselors who avoid supervision do so psychologically, not physically, though there are counselors who avoid by missing or coming late to their supervision sessions.

Bauman has pointed out that counselors can play games to avoid dealing with their skill issues.[10] His frequently cited article outlines some of the postures presented by supervisees that, in effect, help them to avoid supervision. Bauman's list of five "games" is as relevant today as it was when it was published, and includes such strategies as *submission, turning the tables, "I'm no good," helplessness,* and *projection.*

Submission

In the *submission* game, trainees yield immediately to the superior knowledge of the supervisor. Discussion is not warranted because the

[10] William F. Bauman, "Games Counselor Trainees Play: Dealing with Trainee Resistance," *Counselor Education and Supervision* 11, no. 4 (1972): 251–56.

trainee begs out as a result of obvious inferior judgment. He or she accepts all feedback unquestioningly—almost, it seems, before hearing it. Under such conditions, the trainee communicates complete malleability and unaccountability.

Turning the Tables

We alluded to the game of *turning the tables* earlier when we discussed the counselor who solicits the teacher role from the supervisor through extensive questioning. The trainee approaches supervision as an inexhaustible source of answers to an infinite list of questions about what the supervisor suggests could have been done in the previous session. The trainee arrives at supervision well armed—but well armed to keep the supervisor at arm's length rather than well armed to learn.

"I'm No good"

The game of *"I'm no good"* is more active than the submission strategy. Here the trainee must convince the supervisor that he or she is on the verge of becoming a counselor casualty. The trainee magnifies counseling mistakes, placing the supervisor in the role of diminishing those self-deprecating remarks and assuring the trainee that there is hope. One possible consequence of this game is to invite the supervisor into a counselor role.

Helplessness

Yet another variation on the same theme, *helplessness* is a stance protesting lack of experience as a reason for the supervisor to take full responsibility for the direction of the trainee's counseling. In this litigious time in our profession, an increasingly common example of helplessness occurs when the trainee raises the issue of the supervisor's legal responsibility for mistakes made in the counseling session. Helpless trainees can be remarkably resourceful in their arguments.

Projection

Finally, a frequently used avoidance posture is to project the mistakes one has made in counseling onto the supervision process itself. The most salient example of *projection* is when the trainee protests that sessions that are observed by the supervisor are far more stilted and self-conscious than sessions that occur in the absence of the supervisor (or when the tape recorder is turned off). The focus of the supervision session becomes the "imposition" of supervision rather than the trainee's skills. And the message is that, for whatever reason, the supervisor never really sees the trainee's highly developed (or even adequate) counseling skills.

Liddle has asserted that trainee resistance stems from an attempt to avoid a perceived threat. She lists five possible sources of threat in supervision: (1) evaluation anxiety; (2) performance anxiety (living up to one's own standards of performance); (3) personal issues within the supervisee (such as having unresolved feelings about death when counseling a client who is mourning the loss of a loved one); (4) deficits in the supervisory relationship; and (5) anticipated consequences (resisting the learning of how to confront out of fear of client anger).[11]

Does knowing about resistance help to avoid it? How do you overcome those things that threaten you in supervision? First of all, it is essential that you realize and accept that some anxiety in supervision is unavoidable.[12] We could even say that feeling no anxiety is in itself a form of avoidance. Secondly, you must try to identify the sources of your anxiety if you are to resolve them. If you feel yourself avoiding supervision, you might discuss this with your supervisor. Or if that's too threatening, you could find a peer you trust to help you uncover the motives or fears underlying your resistance. Finally, trainees need to find productive ways to handle their resistance rather than succumbing to a psychological avoidance of supervision. For example, pairing some of the ideas presented above, let's say that you are playing helpless with your supervisor out of a fear that learning to confront will cause client anger. Continuing to be helpless is inappropriate. However, it is highly appropriate to acknowledge your fear to your supervisor. Once you and your supervisor are dealing with the real issue, alternative strategies can be suggested. Acknowledging that you cannot counsel forever without needing the skill to confront a client, the supervisor can role play an angry client with you, allowing you to face your fears in a safer environment. Or if it is too threatening even to do this with your supervisor, you can perform the role play with one of your peers, thus gaining some experience in a nonevaluative environment. Just as there are innumerable ways for the creative but anxious trainee to avoid supervision, there are innumerable ways to help trainees conquer their fears, once those fears are accepted as a normal and legitimate part of supervision.[13]

A final caution: You can become as hard on yourself in your demand to be "open" in supervision as you are about your counseling skills. It's okay to hold back a little. Try not to take yourself too seriously. And remember that your supervisor was once in your position.

PREPARING FOR SUPERVISION

Yager and his associates identified tips for maximizing the counselor's time in supervision.[14] Several of their suggestions have been presented in other sections of this chapter. In addition, they offer several guidelines, such as

[11] Becky J. Liddle, "Resistance in Supervision: A Response to Perceived Threat," *Counselor Education and Supervision* 26, no. 2 (1986): 117–27.

[12] Geoffrey G. Yager, Mary V. Witham, George T. Williams, and Carol E. Scheufler, "Tips for the Inexperienced Counselor: How to Maximize Your Time in Supervision" (Paper presented at the North Central Association for Counselor Education and Supervision Annual Meeting, Milwaukee, 1981).

[13] Becky J. Liddle, "Resistance in Supervision."

[14] Geoffrey G. Yager et al., "Tips for the Inexperienced Counselor."

trusting your supervisor as a most critical variable, clarifying for yourself what is most needed from supervision, communicating openly with your supervisor concerning those identified needs, and clarifying with your supervisor the content and format of supervision sessions.

Basic to all of the suggestions listed above is taking responsibility for your own supervision. There is, of course, a paradox in this suggestion, which is why it can be difficult to carry out. By the time trainees come to supervision, they have had a great deal of experience as learners. Usually this experience has taught them that they are to figure out their instructor's game plan as soon as possible and not deviate from that plan. They believe that it is their instructor's responsibility to determine what is to be learned, and that it is desirable for them to think critically within those parameters, but not to step outside the limits set by the instructor.

And yet the need to identify your own learning needs and to be able to evaluate realistically your own performance is critical to successful supervision. A trainee's inability or unwillingness to do this will hamper the supervision process. As a result, supervision represents a transition from classroom learning to professional practice. Therein lies the paradox. The most effective counseling student is the student who stops behaving like a student.

A key way that trainees show their preparedness for supervision is to evaluate themselves before each supervision session. This is equivalent to taking home the test and scoring it yourself before your instructor scores it. Even if the supervisor does not demand it (and many do), trainees should review their audiotapes (or their notes, or their recollections) to determine where supervision is most needed. Supervisors find it frustrating if they feel that they are spending more time reviewing their trainees' sessions than the trainees are. Trainees who come to supervision having prepared a rough draft of their performance evaluation are bound to gain more from the experience.

On a more mundane level, but perhaps almost as important, preparing for supervision involves being organized in all aspects of your counseling. If you plan to present an audiotape to your supervisor, be sure that the tape and the audio recorder work *prior to* the counseling session. If the first ten minutes of the tape are from a former session or do not pertain to what you hope to cover, forward the tape to the appropriate spot, or write a note to go with the tape if the supervisor is to listen to it at a later time. Mark which side of the tape contains the session. Hours and hours have been wasted by frustrated supervisors when such small courtesies have been overlooked. Furthermore, taking control of these small but not insignificant details will give you a sense of control over the entire experience. This will most likely generalize to other aspects of your training experience.

USING SUPERVISION

Just as you should come to supervision prepared to use your time productively, you should leave with a sense of direction. Going back to one of the definitions of supervision, Kutzik emphasized that the supervisor is to provide "direction that the supervisee is bound to follow."[15] It is entirely possible that the supervisor thinks that the implications of supervision are totally clear, but the counselor has no idea how to transfer the information gained in supervision to subsequent counseling sessions. It is even possible that the counselor is not aware that the two (counseling and supervision) should be purposefully connected.

All things being equal, translating supervision to direction for the counselor is a shared responsibility between the supervisor and the trainee. If, however, it is not clear to you how one relates to the other, you should ask before you are expected to perform again. This will avoid a common complaint made by supervisors that certain trainees are enjoyable to work with, but they don't seem to follow through on supervisory suggestions.

Even if it is clear how you are to use a supervisory suggestion, it is wise to prepare yourself sometime after supervision but before your next counseling contact. What seems perfectly clear in a discussion with your supervisor may become muddled or somehow out of reach during the counseling session if you have not integrated the concepts into your own frame of reference prior to the session. This failure to integrate is a common mistake made by trainees, one that causes them unnecessary feelings of discouragement and embarrassment. The key to maximizing supervision is to invest additional energy between supervision and subsequent counseling sessions. This will help you to avoid having to expend energy after the session to recover from disappointment of lack of success.

SUMMARY

We have addressed several of the components of supervision. Only when these operate in unison, however, do we have what is referred to as supervision. Regardless of focus, role, or method, supervision is most often described as the most rewarding part of a counselor's training. Likewise, supervisors report a high degree of satisfaction in their work with supervisees. Both parties are reflecting the distinct pleasure of passing on and safeguarding the profession of counseling.

DISCUSSION QUESTIONS

1. Everyone approaches a new experience with certain expectations. List three things you hoped to receive from supervision. List three things you know that you don't want from supervision. Discuss.

2. Looking over Bauman's list of five "games," which one do you think you are most likely to play? When you are playing this game, what should your supervisor do?

---

[15] Alfred J. Kutzik, "The Medical Field," p. 5.

3. Most trainees receiving live supervision for the first time are nervous about how clients will react to this method. With a partner, role play an explanation of live supervision to a client. Give each other feedback.
4. In a small group, make a list of ways you can prepare for supervision. In a similar fashion, make a list of ways that you can increase the likelihood of using the supervision you receive in subsequent counseling sessions.

RECOMMENDED READINGS

BAUMAN, WILLIAM F.   "Games Counselor Trainees Play: Dealing with Trainee Resistance," *Counselor Education and Supervision* 11 (1972): 251–56.

Bauman describes trainee resistance as five "games" and offers supervision interventions for dealing with each form of resistance.

HAWTHORNE, LILLIAN   "Games Supervisors Play," *Social Work* 20 (1975): 179–83.

Hawthorne turns the tables and considers how supervisors play games. She believes that the reason for supervisor games is the supervisor's difficulty handling authority. She divides supervisor games into games of abdication and games of power.

KADUSHIN, ALFRED   "Games People Play in Supervision," *Social Work* 13 (1968): 23–32.

Similar to Bauman's article, Kadushin sees games as emerging when the student is afraid to change or fears being inadequate. Kadushin categorizes games as: (1) manipulating demand levels; (2) redefining the relationship; (3) reducing power disparity; and (4) controlling the situation. Kadushin also gives some attention to supervisor's "counter-games."

NELSON, GARY L.   "Psychotherapy Supervision from the Trainee's Point of View: A Survey of Preferences," *Professional Psychology* 9 (1978): 539–50.

Nelson reports on a study of several supervisory variables. The most noteworthy results were that trainees preferred live observation and videotaping as the method of supervision and preferred a supervisor who was flexible and interested in having the trainee develop an individualized therapeutic style.

YAGER, GEOFFREY G., AND TERRENCE D. BECK.   "Beginning Practicum: It Only Hurt until I Laughed!" *Counselor Education and Supervision* 25 (1985): 149–57.

Yager and Beck enumerate several types of counselor responses that originate out of concern for competence or fear of intimacy with the client. Inappropriate counselor responses are represented in an exaggerated fashion that allows novice counselors to learn through humor.

APPENDIX

Counseling Strategies Checklist

Most counselor trainees view the opportunity for supervision as a mixed blessing. They know that their performance has "blind spots" that are more easily identified by an observer. On the other hand, they feel vulnerable at the prospect of having someone view and assess their interview behavior, particularly when they cannot see that person. There are no easy solutions to this problem. Learning to feel comfortable with your supervisor is uniquely a function of your own goals and the supervisor's awareness of your discomfort. Therefore, you must identify the implications of your counseling goals in terms of your own risk taking, and you must be prepared to communicate your fears to your supervisor.

The Counseling Strategies Checklist (CSC) is suggested as one means of assessing your performance. It is divided into categories that conform to the skills chapters in this text. The supervisor may want to use parts of the checklist for each interview, rather than attempting to complete the total checklist each time you are observed. The checklist provides a point of departure for you and your supervisor to discuss the progress of the interview, and your input and its effect upon your client.

One further point might be made in reference to the use of the supervisor evaluation. It was mentioned in the text that the counselor often encounters *blocks* while attempting to respond to clients. The counselor may be able to identify quite accurately the feeling the client is describing, but may not be able to respond to that feeling. This would probably be described by the Freudians as countertransference. When the client talks about a problem that is also a problem for the counselor, the counselor may feel unqualified to respond, or may be overwhelmed by personal feelings and unable to respond. It is at this point that a supervisor can be most helpful in counseling the counselor, helping him or her to work through personal feelings, and identifying ways to manage these feelings the next time the situation arises. To receive this assistance from your supervisor, you must acknowledge your own blockage.

How to Use the Counseling Strategies Checklist

Each item in the CSC is scored by circling the most appropriate response, either "Yes," "No," or "N.A." (not applicable). The items are worded so that desirable responses are "Yes" or "N.A." "No" is an undesirable response.

After the supervisor has observed and rated the interview, the two of you should sit down and review the ratings. Where noticeable deficiencies exist, you and the supervisor should identify a goal or goals that will remedy the problem. Beyond this, you should list two or three action steps that permit you to achieve the goal. After three or four more interviews, have the supervisor evaluate you again, and compare the two sets of ratings to determine whether or not progress was evident.

Part I: Counselor Reinforcing Behavior (Nonverbal)

1. The counselor maintained eye contact with the client.

   Yes   No   N.A.

2. The counselor displayed several different facial expressions during the interview.

   Yes   No   N.A.

3. The counselor's facial expressions reflected the mood of the client.

   Yes   No   N.A.

4. The counselor often responded to the client with facial animation and alertness.

   Yes   No   N.A.

5. The counselor displayed intermittent head movements (up-down, side-to-side).

   Yes   No   N.A.

6. The counselor refrained from head nodding when the client did not pursue goal-directed topics.

   Yes   No   N.A.

7. The counselor demonstrated a relaxed body position.

   Yes   No   N.A.

8. The counselor leaned forward as a means of encouraging the client to engage in some goal-directed behavior.

   Yes   No   N.A.

9. The counselor demonstrated some variation in voice pitch when talking.

   Yes   No   N.A.

10. The counselor's voice was easily heard by the client.

    Yes   No   N.A.

11. The counselor used intermittent one-word vocalizations ("mm-hmm") to reinforce the client's demonstration of goal-directed topics or behaviors.

    Yes   No   N.A.

Counselor Reinforcing Behavior (Verbal)

12. The counselor usually spoke slowly enough so that each word was easily understood.

    Yes   No   N.A.

13. A majority (60 percent or more) of the counselor's responses could be categorized as complete sentences rather than monosyllabic phrases.

    Yes   No   N.A.

14. The counselor's verbal statements were concise and to the point.

    Yes   No   N.A.

15. The counselor refrained from repetition in verbal statements.

    Yes   No   N.A.

16. The counselor made verbal comments that pursued the topic introduced by the client.

    Yes   No   N.A.

17. The subject of the counselor's verbal statements usually referred to the client, either by name or the second-person pronoun, "you."

    Yes   No   N.A.

18. A clear and sensible progression of topics was evident in the counselor's verbal behavior; the counselor avoided rambling.

Yes   No   N.A.

Part II: Opening the Interview

1. In the first part of the interview, the counselor used several different nonverbal gestures (smiling, head nodding, hand movement, etc.) to help put the client at ease.

Yes   No   N.A.

2. In starting the interview the counselor remained silent or invited the client to talk about whatever he or she wanted, thus leaving the selection of initial topic up to the client.

Yes   No   N.A.

3. After the first five minutes of the interview, the counselor refrained from encouraging social conversation.

Yes   No   N.A.

4. After the first topic of discussion was exhausted, the counselor remained silent until the client identified a new topic.

Yes   No   N.A.

5. The counselor provided structure (information about nature, purposes of counseling, time limits, etc.) when the client indicated uncertainty about the interview.

Yes   No   N.A.

6. In beginning the *initial* interview, the counselor used at least one of the following structuring procedures:
   a. Provided information about taping and/or observation
   b. Commented on confidentiality
   c. Made remarks about the counselor's role and purpose of the interview
   d. Discussed with the client his or her expectations about counseling

Yes   No   N.A.

Part III: Termination of the Interview

1. The counselor informed the client before terminating that the interview was almost over.

Yes   No   N.A.

2. The counselor refrained from introducing new material (a different topic) at the termination phase of the interview.

   Yes   No   N.A.

3. The counselor discouraged the client from pursuing new topics within the last five minutes of the interview by avoiding asking for further information about it.

   Yes   No   N.A.

4. Only one attempt to terminate the interview was required before the termination was actually completed.

   Yes   No   N.A.

5. The counselor initiated the termination of the interview through use of some closing strategy such as acknowledgment of time limits and/or summarization (by self or client).

   Yes   No   N.A.

6. At the end of the interview, the counselor offered the client an opportunity to return for another interview.

   Yes   No   N.A.

Part IV: Goal Setting

1. The counselor asked the client to identify some of the conditions surrounding the occurrence of the client's problem (*"When* do you feel_____?").

   Yes   No   N.A.

2. The counselor asked the client to identify some of the consequences resulting from the client's behavior ("What happens when you_____?").

   Yes   No   N.A.

3. The counselor asked the client to state how he or she would like to change his or her behavior. ("How would you like for things to be different?").

   Yes   No   N.A.

4. The counselor and client decided *together* upon counseling goals.

   Yes   No   N.A.

5. The goals set in the interview were specific and observable.

   Yes   No   N.A.

6. The counselor asked the client to orally state a commitment to work for goal achievement.

   Yes   No   N.A.

7. If the client appeared resistant or unconcerned about achieving change, the counselor discussed this with the client.

   Yes   No   N.A.

8. The counselor asked the client to specify at least one action step he or she might take toward his or her goal.

   Yes   No   N.A.

9. The counselor suggested alternatives available to the client.

   Yes   No   N.A.

10. The counselor helped the client to develop action steps for goal attainment.

    Yes   No   N.A.

11. Action steps designated by counselor and client were specific and realistic in scope.

    Yes   No   N.A.

12. The counselor provided an opportunity within the interview for the client to practice or rehearse the action step.

    Yes   No   N.A.

13. The counselor provided feedback to the client concerning the execution of the action step.

    Yes   No   N.A.

14. The counselor encouraged the client to observe and evaluate the progress and outcomes of action steps taken outside the interview.

    Yes   No   N.A.

Part V: Counselor Discrimination

1. The counselor's responses were usually directed toward the most important component of *each* of the client's communications.

   Yes   No   N.A.

2. The counselor followed client topic changes by responding to the primary cognitive or affective idea reflecting a common theme in each communication.

   Yes   No   N.A.

3. The counselor usually identified and responded to the feelings of the client.

   Yes   No   N.A.

4. The counselor usually identified and responded to the behaviors of the client.

   Yes   No   N.A.

5. The counselor verbally acknowledged several (at least two) nonverbal affect cues.

   Yes   No   N.A.

6. The counselor encouraged the client to talk about his or her feelings.

   Yes   No   N.A.

7. The counselor encouraged the client to identify and evaluate his or her actions.

   Yes   No   N.A.

8. The counselor discouraged the client from making and accepting excuses (rationalization) for his or her behavior.

   Yes   No   N.A.

9. The counselor asked questions that the client couldn't answer in a yes or no fashion (typically beginning with words such as *how, what, when, where, who,* etc.).

   Yes   No   N.A.

10. Several times (at least two) the counselor confronted the client with a discrepancy present in the client's communication and/or behavior.

    Yes   No   N.A.

11. Several times (at least two) the counselor used responses that supported or reinforced something the client said or did.

    Yes   No   N.A.

12. The counselor used several (at least two) responses that suggested a course of action the client had the potential for completing in the future.

    Yes   No   N.A.

13. Sometimes the counselor restated or clarified the client's previous communication.

    Yes   No   N.A.

14. The counselor used several (at least two) responses that summarized ambivalent and conflicting feelings of the client.

    Yes   No   N.A.

15. The counselor encouraged discussion of negative feelings (anger, fear) expressed by the client.

    Yes   No   N.A.

16. Several times (at least two) the counselor suggested how the client might feel about a particular topic.

    Yes   No   N.A.

Part VI: The Process of Relating

1. The counselor made statements that reflected the client's feelings.

   Yes   No   N.A.

2. The counselor responded to the core of a long and ambivalent client statement.

   Yes   No   N.A.

3. The counselor verbally stated his or her desire and/or intent to understand.

   Yes   No   N.A.

4. The counselor made verbal statements that the client reaffirmed without qualifying or changing the counselor's previous response.

   Yes   No   N.A.

5. The counselor made attempts to verbally communicate his or her understanding of the client that elicited an affirmative client resposne ("Yes, that's exactly right," and so forth).

   Yes   No   N.A.

6. The counselor reflected the client's feelings at the same or a greater level of intensity than originally expressed by the client.

   Yes   No   N.A.

7. In communicating understanding of the client's feelings, the counselor verbalized the anticipation present in the client's communication (i.e., what the client would like to do or how the client would like to be).

   Yes   No   N.A.

8. The counselor frowned when failing to understand what the client was saying.

   Yes   No   N.A.

9. The counselor verbalized personal confusion or misunderstanding to the client.

   Yes   No   N.A.

10. The counselor nodded when agreeing with or encouraging the client.

    Yes   No   N.A.

11. When the counselor's nonverbal behavior suggested that he or she was uncertain or disagreeing, the counselor verbally acknowledged this to the client.

    Yes   No   N.A.

12. The counselor answered directly when the client asked about his or her opinion or reaction.

    Yes   No   N.A.

13. The counselor encouraged discussion of statements made by the client that challenged the counselor's knowledge and beliefs.

    Yes   No   N.A.

14. Several times (at least twice) the counselor shared his or her own feelings with the client.

    Yes   No   N.A.

15. At least one time during the interview the counselor provided specific feedback to the client.

    Yes   No   N.A.

16. The counselor encouraged the client to identify and discuss his or her feelings concerning the counselor and the interview.

    Yes   No   N.A.

17. The counselor voluntarily shared his or her feelings about the client and the counseling relationship.

    Yes   No   N.A.

18. The counselor expressed reactions about the client's strengths and/or potential.

    Yes   No   N.A.

19. The counselor made responses that reflected his or her liking and appreciation of the client.

    Yes   No   N.A.

Index

Nonverbal behavior, 171–72
  acknowledgement response, 54, 56
  affect cues, 81–82, 86
Nurturance, 19

Outcome goals:
  distinguished from process goals, 110–11
  elements of good, 112
  exercise in, 112–13
  outlining, 115–16
  (See also Goals; Goal setting)
Outplacement counseling service, 7
Overparticipation, 40, 41

Pain, 84
Paraprofessional counselors, 4
Personalization skills, 155, 156–58
Phenomenological approach, 96
Phillips, Susan D., 38
Physical needs, 107
Pine, Gerald J., 13, 38
Positive affect, 82–83
Positive regard, 13, 17–19, 40, 88
Premack principle, 146
Probes, 54, 56, 73–74
Problem conceptualization, 106–10
Process goals, distinguished from outcome goals, 110
Process skills, 155–56, 158
Professional helpers, defined, 4
Professional skills, 155, 157–58
Projection, 165

Quarrelsomeness, 83

Rational-emotive therapy, 96, 138
Reflection-of-feeling response, 54, 55, 88
Rehabilitation counseling, 8
Rehearsal strategies, 132, 135–38
Relaxation, 34
Religious counselors, 6–7
Request for clarification, 54, 55–57
Resistance, to goal setting, 116–17
Restatements, 54–55, 72–73, 88
Rewards, from self, 145–47
Ritualized communication patterns, 39
Rogers, Carl, 2, 13, 14, 17, 19
Role-play strategies, 132–38
  conflict resolution and self-awareness and, 133–34
  dialoguing, 134–35
  role reversal, 132–33
Role reversal, 23, 132–33

Sadness, 82, 85–86
School counselors, 5
Selective reinforcement, 76–77
Self-actualization, 111
Self-awareness, 133–34
Self-contracting, 147
Self-disclosure, 22–26, 135–36
Self-esteem needs, 107
Self-management, 142–48
Self-monitoring, 142–45
Self-reporting, 162
Self-reward, 145–47
Sex, need for, 107

Sharing, feedback and, 24–26
Silence, 43–47
  client-induced, 45–46
  counselor-induced, 44–45
  as discriminative stimulus, 72
  therapeutic, 46
Silent caring, 47
Silent focusing, 46
Simek-Downing, Lynn, 27
Simulation, 163–64
Skill training, 137–38
Smiles, 33
Social modeling, 128–32
  characteristics of, 130
  exercise, 131–32
  procedures, 128–30
Status needs, 107
Stevic, Richard R., 14, 17
Strategies (see Counseling strategies)
Subgoals, 114
Submission, 164–65
Success needs, 107
Summarization, interview termination and, 61–62
Summarization-of-feelings response, 54, 55, 90–91
Supervision, 153–69
  avoidance of, 164–66
  conceptualization skills, 155, 156
  Counseling Strategies Checklist and, 170–71
  group, 164
  methods of, 162–64
  parameters of, 153–55
  personalization skills, 155, 156–58
  preparation for, 166–67
  process skills, 155–56, 158
  professional skills, 155, 157–58
  styles of, 159–62
  use of, 167–68
Survival needs, 107
Symbolic modeling, 129

Teacher role, supervisor in, 159–60, 161
Termination:
  of counseling relationship, 63–66
  of interview, 60–63, 173–74
Tharp, R., 143
Thoresen, C. E., 113, 143
Thought stopping, 139–40
Truax, Charles B., 19–20

Underparticipation, 40–41
Unstructured invitations, 52–53

Verbal behavior, 172–73
  affect cues, 81–87
  attentiveness and, 31, 35–36
  minimal, 72
  responses to affective contents, 88–93
Videotape, 163
Vocal characteristics, 35–36, 84, 85

Warner, Richard W., Jr., 14, 17
Watson, D., 143

Yager, Geoffrey G., 166